DREAMS

EXPLORING UNCHARTED DEPTHS OF CONSCIOUSNESS

Mary Phelan

Disclaimer

This book is an account of the author's journey of self-analysis through dreams. It is hoped the reader will find the methods and meanings she discovered during the journey applicable for their own lives, but this is entirely at their own risk and on their own cognisance. The information in this book should not be used as a substitute for professional advice. Neither the author or publisher can be held responsible for any loss, claim or damage arising out of the use, or misuse of the suggestions made, the failure to take professional advice or for any material on third party websites.

Dreams provide you with your future visions;
reality enables you to pin that vision in place.....

Contents

How to use this book

The Children of an Idle Brain is divided into roughly two sections, the "why" and the "how". The "why" part of the book begins with my **Introduction**, in which I explain the physiology of dreaming and stress why adequate sleep is essential for both physical and mental health. In subsequent chapters, I provide information on historical approaches to dream analysis, including notes on Aristotle, Von Leibniz, Sigmund Freud and Carl Jung, and other information. In the "how" part of the book, I provide information upon how to establish dream archetypes, together with post-dream meditative exercises to assist with this process. The remainder of the book is essentially a compendium of categorised dream symbols, which I have divided into "**The Concrete World**", "**The Natural World**", "**Journeys Energy Travel**", and so on. A glossary of dream terms and a table of dream archetypes complete the book. The reader may benefit from dipping into the chapters at random, for example, **Meditative Exercises**, since an understanding of each one does not rely on knowledge gained in the one preceding it. However, I imagine that the majority of readers will gain the most satisfaction by beginning at the beginning, and absorbing the entire history of this most fascinating of subjects.

Why I have written this book

For years I wondered: why do certain people always seem to make the right decisions - or come out on top, even following many wrong turnings? Why do some people seem to have bags of career success and money, while others spend their lives scraping spare change together for the most basic of things? The same puzzling questions applied to relationships and even, gambling with small amounts of money. Why do certain business people always seem to win the big and exciting deals, while others eventually are forced to put up the "for sale" sign? The answer, like all of the best answers, came to me gradually. These people, whether by accident or design, had learned how to get in touch with that inner something, that little voice unheard by anyone else that warns us of both danger and opportunity – *before* these things happened.

The majority of you reading this book will certainly have a major ambition; else you would not be reading it. In view of this ambition, you will most likely have a combination of academic qualifications, work experiences and career contacts to bring you closer to your goal. However, no matter how hard you try, no matter how many times you have approached the brink of achievement, no matter what progress you have made, something always happens along and steals the moment.

THOSE INFURIATING NEARLY-THERE'S

For example, you may have landed a great and wonderful job in an organisation that you have always wanted an association with and - the next thing, you have found yourself in the company of a cantankerous colleague or manager, someone who is determined to bring you down.

Or the company fortunes took a downturn just when you were on the brink of success and you lost your post. I'm not talking theoretically; these things have happened to me. I, too, learned about *the nearly there* and lost it, not once but many times. No matter how far I travelled, no matter how much progress I had made, gremlins invariably popped up to spoil and steal the prize that should have been mine; a loathsome boss appeared out of the smoke, determined rivals hotly contested the job that I desperately wanted or family trouble got in the way. My own life was so littered with might-have-beens and if-onlys, that there were times I wondered what this life was all about. The remedy, I believed, lay between the covers of books. So, I read many books with titles that read like "be master of your own destiny" and "take control of your life", and other similar titles. But – the happenings kept on happening. Over time, I found that even when I followed authorial instructions to the letter, achieving success was never as easy as the experts made it out to be. No matter how many experts bleated the blue skies' philosophy, there always seemed to be a spanner stuck in the way of success and me.

Most infuriating were those tomes that considered success – or lack of it – a moral issue. I have clenched my teeth over many a text – I can't name any for fear of lawsuits – spelling out that success and failure are down to *personal choice*, that if you really wanted to be successful then you would be, that failure is another word for laziness, and so on – well, I now say grrr to all of that! One good thing came of this constant breast-beating; in spite of my helplessness, I felt obliged to work out the difference between what I really could control and the circumstances that I could not avoid. What I discovered was enlightening and empowering.

Ultimately, we can't control our environment, which encompasses the behaviour of other people, traffic jams, industrial action and the weather. Over time I learned that the only thing that I – or you, or anyone else – can ever really take control of, is our own behaviour. This is true at every level of life, and applies to everyone, tycoon or tea-maker. It is for people like me that I wrote this book, people who have discovered that we can't "arrange" to be successful any more than we can arrange for tomorrow to be a fine day. By "success" I mean, of course, whatever your dream or goal is. The exercises and advice that follow do not highlight one career or attainment level over another. Success is what *you* want in life, and everyone's role has equal merit.

I have already stated that the majority of this book's readers will have a defined goal in life and will have taken steps to get there. It is not difficult to takes these steps; you can prepare to excel in a discipline or follow a particular profession through study and training. The better prepared you are, the greater will be your chance of success when an opportunity happens along. You *know* that somewhere is a solution to your problem or, at least, a way forward. But the problem is, you don't know which route to take or who to turn to.

It is a paradox, but it is far easier to visualize a grand, distant goal than to work your way around the petty annoyances that seem to spring up each time you begin to make a move to get there. The problem lies in knowing which of those minor options to choose, options that seem of no consequence when you choose them but do make a marked difference at a further stage of progress. Many books have been printed about these obstacles, of course, with titles like "time management for better living" or "how to say no and mean it", "ten tips for better negotiating" or "relationships and work: how to balance your life". All narratives are valid and yet…

As I scanned the bookshelves and saw titles like these, I felt a lack, an awareness that something was missing. Knowing how to manage time, negotiate deals and achieve a truce with any partner were great skills, but not one book that I found helped me deal with the essential me. Again, books on these and similar topics proliferate, books on how to increase your awareness and intuition, on meditation and hypnosis. For a number of years, I had great fun applying the principles, trying to apply the lessons learned to mundane situations, all in practice for the Big Decisions. And for a while, the examined life did seem to work for me. I did college courses and acquired qualifications and made baby steps towards getting into editorial and advertising. But I was not happy; obstacles were always standing in the way of me and the big time.

Then, a number of years ago, I had a dream that I was standing in an employment bureau. A man was seated beside a typewriter, and I was telling him that I just *had* to find a job as a copywriter. I quote: 'it's my identity; it's who I am.' Immediately, I awoke with a strong sense of yearning that stayed with me until I got my first copywriting assignment – and I still experience that feeling, both while waking and dreaming. And when I do get the feeling, I just know that I have to act upon it, a situation that has led to my recording *all* of my dreams.

Over the past eleven years, this recording has taken discipline and time, but the effort has been worth it. The fact is, I do *not* dream the same dreams all of the time. And from listening to other people on the same subject, neither do they. Not alone that, I have had precognitive dream experiences so astonishing that even now, they make my jaw drop. But more important than any precognition is what I have learned about *me*, through dream analysis, the exploration of dream symbols, mining information about my life, how fears and hopes come disguised in dream imagery, and how I have dealt with so many problems by just listening in to the voice that speaks to you while I sleep.

I have learned that dream analysis allows us to take hold of the reins sooner and accelerate the maturation process. Those "strange" subjects who appear in your dreams are the variegated facets of your own personality. Recognition and identification are precursors to the glorious control that hails personal maturity.

In addition, dream analysis has made me more aware of the "real" environment, of how to intuit other peoples' moods – a craft that has yielded much fruit - and all of this is without mentioning the rich harvest of creative material that I have turned into works of fiction and other books. In truth, dream analysis – once you master the craft – is akin to opening Aladdin's cave, gaining access to the fascinating aspects of your own personality.

In this book, I explain why dream interpretation is the gateway to the subconscious, that hidden store of thoughts and ideas, of solutions to problems that seem to have no solution until you suddenly find the answer, throughout waking hours. I explore the different levels of consciousness and explain why what resides in the subconscious is just as valid, in many cases much more so, as any thoughts that we might experience throughout waking hours. I explain how to "capture" dreams and use them as material for creative exercises and problem-solving.

I lay out the physiology of dreaming, explaining why this function is vital to our psychological health and well-being. Sufficient sleep is, of course, vital to good physical health, which implies that dreaming is essential to the well-balanced personality. Be aware, from the outset, that this book is not just another re-hash of Freudian or Jungian dream theory, filled with notes on wish fulfilment and repressed sexuality. When I mention those two gentlemen at all, it is to put their theories, and those of other dream theorists, in the context of the history of dream interpretation. This discipline, like all others, has a history, one that I believe is important for the reader to understand in order to see how far the art of dream interpretation has travelled in the past hundred or so years.

I explore the topic of dream archetypes and instruct the dreamer on how to identify archetypes that will help him during his waking hours. I provide numerous dream scenarios and interpretations and show how the reader can adapt these in order to accurately interpret his own dreams. In addition, I provide meditative exercises that may provide a bridge to the subconscious during waking hours. I finish this volume with a glossary of words to help the reader through the more obscure science of sleep and dreaming, and the table of archetypes that I have gathered over the years. Overall, my aim is to show the reader how to build a roadmap to follow during waking hours, a guide to where to manoeuvre next, and of how to avoid all that is irksome and unnecessary. And I believe that dream analysis makes us better, happier and more prosperous people, willing to contribute to the common good. In summary, welcome to the wonderful world of sleep-time dreaming.

Introduction

The notion of dreaming is one that has ever drawn snorts of derision from many "practical" people, whether the dreamer be awake or asleep. *Don't be dreaming,* my elders would say, whenever I expressed a wish to do or have or achieve something spectacular – or even relatively banal. With the passing years, many of my dreams have taken on a stubborn solidity, and my only wish now is that I had had more witnesses to how I discovered the power of how dreaming *in combination with taking action* can transform your life. That last bit is important; without action, you cannot expect to achieve anything. No matter how hopeless life seems, you must keep trying.

Here, I pause to ask how many travellers can see their destinations before embarking on their journeys? The end of the trip may be disappointing, but that is no reason for not beginning the voyage. For the person who does not have a goal, in the sense that he does not know what to do with his life, analysing the archetypes that express themselves in his night-time phantasms are a good way of pinpointing of what is truly significant to him. Such self-knowledge often surprises the dreamer. What you discover won't always be reassuring or comforting but it will be authentic and empowering – and power is what we are after here.

THE POWER OF SELF-KNOWLEDGE

In the same way that the majority of us keep our "real" selves hidden from public view, we only get the occasional waking glimpse of much that is "true" about ourselves. Dream analysis goes a long way to collecting the missing pieces of the picture. Great psychologists like

Sigmund Freud and Carl Jung knew this, which is why their psychoanalytic methods involved bringing the subject in touch with his subconscious. The reason that this information arrives disguised as dream imagery is that your growing maturity is a journey that brings you closer to discovering where your subconscious may be trying to guide you. Learning how to uncover this hidden material is essential to growth in the personality. If you "understood" everything surrounding yourself too early in life, your lack of maturity would cause you to bleat about it too soon, and much of this rich material would be squandered or lost forever.

And growing maturity should go hand-in-hand with understanding the material sent us by our subconscious. Understand this now: certain members of the population have the knack of doing everything correctly. These are the people that I alluded to earlier, the people who always seem to know in advance of good fortune what move to make, who to work for, what neighbourhood to live in, what friends to make. I repeat: these people, whether by accident or design, have learned how to get in touch with that inner something, that little voice unheard by anyone else that warns us of both danger and opportunity – *before* these things happen along. Many of these people may claim never, ever to have interpreted a dream, that they just got lucky or were very, very good at what they did. And they are probably telling the truth.

But experience has taught me that no one ever gets something for nothing. Somehow, somewhere, successful people have learned that competency, hard work and even, extraordinary talent do not ensure success alone or all together. Chance – or what seems to be chance – does play a part in success. Somehow, somewhere, these successful people have learned to max their opportunities and personal contacts – and I do not believe that this process happens by chance.

THE DANGER OF LEAVING IT TO CHANCE

I am not and never have been an advocate of gambling or any game of chance; however, life often seems to offer much to the lucky man. But our subconscious offers us a store of material that we can learn to connect with, to reduce the instances of where we feel, when confronted with an opportunity or a problem, bound to "guess" what to do next. Many people *never* learn to connect with or understand this store of material, and thus lose a valuable tool when confronted with a problem in life. In many cases, the personality breaks down, and the person needs a trained psychoanalyst or psychologist to step in to help the subject get in touch with his personality again.

Though I do not practise either of those disciplines, I have long noticed that the most realistic of people are those who listen to their dreams, both sleeping and waking, and follow them. According to Bruno Bettelheim: "Independence and transcending childhood require personality development, not becoming better at a particular task, or doing battle with external difficulties".[1]

In other words, you can be the "best" at everything. You may go out into the world and win contracts and slay dragons. But unless you are blessed at birth with innate wisdom, even you may falter now and then when you have gone far towards attaining your goals.

I am aware of other ways to connect with the subconscious, for example, by meditating, undergoing great physical feats, spending days, weeks or even months alone. However, for a variety of reasons, many of these techniques may not suit everyone. But everyone alive does – or should – partake of a life-replenishing sleep, every night. Why not use the material given to you routinely at nighttime, by your subconscious? In this book, I explore *levels of consciousness*, because I

---

1   Bruno Bettelheim, *The Uses of Enchantment: The Meaning and Importance of Fairy Tales* (Penguin: London, 1991), p. 142.

believe that an understanding of these is vital, in the same way as the visitor knows – or not – which level or floor of the building the room that he is seeking, is situated. Be aware that this book is not a manual on how to achieve the forms of higher consciousness available to those who undergo lengthy periods in transcendental meditation and other exercises. My aim is to help the reader attain more ready access to the creative state, which is indeed a type of "higher" consciousness. But following my exercises will not transform you into a mystic or a guru, though I do refer to these states in my chapter, **Levels of Consciousness**, to place dreaming and creativity in context.

Of course, dream analysis without a store of dream material to work upon is not possible and in the text that follows, I comment much on how to capture dreams, a discipline vital to effective dream analysis. Quality dreaming is intimately connected to quality sleep and I stress over and again the importance of a good sleep, every night. The most comprehensive section of the book is filled with numerous, common dream scenarios and instructions on how you might make use of them in your waking life.

I take you through the world of dream archetypes, and provide a section explaining how to identify them, showing how dream-time friends can help you through many a waking hour. And I stress again and again, the importance of taking action – because action is all important. Here, I introduce the notion of the classical and the romantic. Hear the word *classical* and one thinks of a grand building complete with pillars and columns, and rectangular windows. Outside the world of architecture, *classical* is an attitude to life, an orderly and complete way of thinking about and doing things. It is classical action that sets matters in stone following a period of speculating, thinking and planning.

However, the grandest building that ever was could not have come into being without another mode of thought, which is where the *romantic* comes in.

TS Eliot described the rift between the classical and the romantic as: "the difference between the complete and the fragmentary, the adult and the immature, the orderly and the chaotic".[2] Stated this way, we can see that the form of the dream is the essence of romantic thinking, those fragmentary, half-formed ideas and imagery following upon one another, during the hours of sleep.

As an example, consider the dream that I call my Manhattan dream, which took place several years ago, when I was right down in my luck. In the dream, I was living in the centre of Manhattan, acutely aware of my poor fortune. My surroundings were very beautiful; tall, glass towers in a red-tinged, grey sky. It was coming up to Christmas and my only asset was flowing locks of beautiful, blonde hair, not what I have in reality. Other people in the building were using the lift to go up and down. I was in the lift with a male friend when two celebrities, one male and one female, came in.

The man was carrying a leather satchel and the lift went up. The celebrities left at one point, leaving a number of items on the floor, which by now was grown with grass. One item was a piece of plastic, shaped like a spade. I stared at it, feeling miserable and confused.

On analysis, I found that the tall, glass towers with the elevators represented the *ups and downs of life*. The satchel represented *life's bounty*. The male friend was the *masculine side of me,* and the female, was of course, me. The celebrities arrived to show that *success was still possible.* The lush, blonde hair was an indicator that *my assets may have been greater than I thought.* The lift going up was a sign that *things were getting better.* The spade was an indicator that *I would still have to work to get what I wanted.*

Not long afterwards, an opportunity presented itself. And two years later again, I was working as an online copywriter. I had also won a

---

2   David Wright, (ed), 'Introduction' in *English Romantic Verse* (London: Penguin Books, 1968), p. xii.

minor prize for journalism. Overall, things were getting better. It is important to remember that your dreams indicate what you believe about you. There is no such thing as something for nothing and to be successful, you will need to work as hard at your profession as you believe yourself to be worthy of success. In order to derive maximum benefit from your dream analysis, you do need to identify dream archetypes and I provide a section in which I explain how to effectively do this. Finally, I provide a dream glossary, an index of all of those words that you hear and see with regard to dreams. But – for every "how" there is a "why". Before I venture into these deeper waters, I explain what a dream is and why we all spend time dreaming.

WHAT IS A DREAM?

A dream is an image or series of images that rise – apparently uninvited - to the surface of our consciousness, usually shortly before we awaken. This dream imagery sometimes manifests when we are trying to fall asleep or even, when we are awake. Most imagery is in the form of an image or series of images, not unlike a film montage. However, it is not unknown for the dreamer to hear sound imagery.

Physiologically, that is what a dream is. Philosophically, it is so much more, a distillation of memories and experiences, fears and hopes, concatenated into a coded cocktail of images that appear to us in our sleep, images that often amuse, frighten or intrigue us, often long into our waking hours. My aim in writing this book is to lead the reader through the world of dream imagery, looking at their cause, examining theory about dreams and dreaming, affirming facts and busting myths and ultimately, exploring ways to use dream material creatively to build a better personal, environment. From Aristotle to Shakespeare, through to Freud and Jung, sages and philosophers throughout the ages have had much to say about dreams and dreaming, and we will look at these, also. First, I am going to establish *how* we dream.

HOW DO WE DREAM?

If you have ever observed your pet dog or cat while he or she sleeps, you may have noticed that at intervals, the eyes seem to jerk rapidly underneath the furry lids in bouts that last for several minutes. During the 1950s, scientists Nathaniel Kleitman, E Aserinsky and W Dement used EEG equipment to establish the various wave frequencies given off by the mammalian brain throughout different states of consciousness, including sleep.[3] Subsequent research in sleep clinics established that this REM or rapid-eye-movement phase of sleep takes place when the subject is most likely to experience bouts of vivid dreaming.[4]

When we fall asleep in the earliest part of the night, we shut our eyes and fall into a deep sleep that lasts between 90 and 100 minutes, a phase known as NREM or non-synchronized sleep. For the next 10 to 20 minutes, the brain stem gives off pulses of electrical activity, pulses that shift eventually to the primary visual cortex, the area of the brain that controls the eyes. At this point, the body loses muscle tone, which is a condition known as atonia. Curiously, when this happens, the mind is in a state of semi-wakefulness.

It is at this phase of sleep that the eyes of the subject begin to move rapidly underneath the lids. Incidentally, the REM phase is not a function of vision, since babies, foetuses and people without sight, experience it. When the REM phase is over, the subject enters another 90-100 minute sleep cycle, that is, about 90 minutes of NREM sleep, followed by 10 or so minutes of REM. Clinical trials have established that on awakening, the majority of subjects are experiencing dreams during this REM time and experience few dreams during the NREM

---

3   Ian Oswald, 'Dreaming' ed. by Richard L Gregory, *The Oxford Companion to the Mind*, (Oxford: Oxford University Press, 1987), p. 201.

4   Oswald, 'Dreaming', *Oxford Companion*, p.202.

phase. The healthy sleeper takes between six and eight hours sleep per night, and so experiences four to eight sleep cycles. As the night advances, the amount of NREM or deep sleep within a cycle decreases, with a correlated increase in the amount of REM or dreaming sleep. This explains why we experience our most vivid dreams towards morning. These discoveries have given sleep psychologists access to material that would otherwise be lost.

Sleep clinics monitor the eye movements of its experimental subjects, and by enabling psychologists to connect dreaming patterns with the mental state of the patient and gain insights into the functions of the mammalian brain, recover material that is useful for purposes including medical diagnosis. What our pets dream about, we can only conjecture but, the next time that he or she awakens after a hard day's sleep I am sure your dog or cat would not object to a helping of roast beef or possibly, mouse.

WHY WE DREAM?

Of course, this medical theory only explains the functioning of the brain's mechanism for providing us with dreams. It does not explain *why* the higher animals, that is, mammals with a brain, produce such a montage of imagery when the brain is in the REM phase. What is apparent is the effect that dreaming has upon the sleeper.

Over time, I have found that dreaming acts as a form of mental caretaking, a kind of psychological holiday from daytime cares. Dreams act as a mental vacation, enabling us to access places and points of view inaccessible during conscious hours. While we are awake, our thoughts are hidebound by convention and cultural habitude. This inhibition vanishes during sleep and in our dreams; we experience surprising and even shocking events that our waking selves could never accept, for example, finding ourselves naked in a room filled with people.

SOLVING PROBLEMS

Those absurd situations we experience in dreams are the subconscious mechanism sending us a disguised solution to a current conundrum. Sometimes, we can access this information without extensive dream analysis. How often when you have had a seemingly unsolvable problem, have you been advised to "sleep on it" – and have woken up with the solution to the problem in your mind? For example, I recently had a problem with an item of household machinery that had slipped out of place and just would not fit back where it belonged. On awakening the day after it broke, I had a sudden vision of soap repairing the mechanism. Later, I tried the method – and it worked! It might sound trite, but it did save me a sum of cash.

Information received at this level is indeed a gift, but it is still worth learning how to analyse dream material that might otherwise prove misleading. For example, a dream of seeing a friend or lover lying in a coffin while you party away with another group of friends might not be an indication that you are all heartless and cruel – or even that said friend/lover is going to die. It could mean that the friend or lover is experiencing the end of something in his or her life, and that you and other friends have many reasons to feel good about it. We don't often receive a literal view of events because our thoughts and feelings are too precious to expose to other people. Our subconscious wants us to probe more deeply, and this probing serves another function.

A SPRINGBOARD TO NEW IDEAS

The world is awash with tales of artists who have created their greatest works and scientists who have made world-changing discoveries by following directions received during the dreamtime. Be it song lyrics or story lines, the blueprints of useful machines or unknown molecular structures, the best treasures always lie hidden from view. The path to professional success may be in the imagery you receive at night; think of dream creativity as mining for gold.

Newly ensconced in Strawberry Hill, his Gothic villa in Twickenham, Horace Walpole dreamed that the helmet of a suit of armour – in reality, furnishing his staircase – fell upon and crushed him. In 1764, Walpole wrote *The Castle of Otranto*, sparking the fashion for what we call Gothic novels. At the heart of the typical Gothic novel is a maiden in peril, mysterious documents, coffins in the crypts and bats in the belfries of rambling, ruined castles and of course, the supernatural. Exactly fifty-two years later, a young woman named Mary Shelley dreamed of a creature composed of pieces of dead men and brought to life by its mad-scientist creator. Today, the myriad movies and plays, spin-offs and send-ups that incorporate the name "Frankenstein" attest to the success of the story. Shelley's narrative, of course, marked the beginning of the science fiction novel. Late in the nineteenth century, a young Scottish writer named Robert Louis Stevenson found that he had the ability to dream entire story plots, dreaming them in portions, waking up and writing them down, and falling asleep again to resume where the plot left off. Today, we have the fabulous *Dr Jekyll and Mr Hyde* as a testimony to this extraordinary talent.[5] And now, science fiction is a significant literary genre. And there is nothing to prevent any subject alive from combining fragments of dream imagery to create the next trend in world literature…..and if only it were that simple?

The dreaming subject must be canny enough to recognize the potential of the nocturnal imagery sent him by his subconscious. The writer must have the guts and will power to sit down for the requisite hours (or days or weeks or years) that it takes to grind out a coherent

5   C Maxwell Cade & Nona Coxhead, *The Awakened Mind: Biofeedback and the Development of Higher States of Awareness* (Dorset: Element Books, 1989), p. 124.

tale from said fragments, and go through the final agony of putting it on the market!

And many informational dreams are the *result* of hard work. In the nineteenth century, Friedrich Kekule von Stradonitz had puzzled over the atomic configuration of the benzene molecule. Following many years spent in study, making notes and trying to make his findings fit current molecular theory, he fell asleep and dreamed of a snake swallowing its tail. On awakening, he had solved the puzzle; the benzene molecule has a *ring* formation.[6] Elias Howe wanted to patent his idea for a sewing machine, but he did not know how to thread the needle. He tried again and again to make his invention work, but simply could not. In a dream, he saw a troupe of warriors carrying spears with holes just below the spear tip, evident on all of the sewing machines available today.

Of course, both Kekule and Howe had to work hard in order to get their findings across, but from these tales, it is evident that dreaming and taking action work in unison. Because our notions of what dreams are and what they can do for us have evolved through the ages, it is both useful and fascinating to explore the evolution of dream theory.

---

6   Cade and Coxhead, *The Awakened Mind*, p. 125.

The Philosophy of Dreaming

Man has always been intrigued by dreams and dreaming. In the ancient world, shamans believed that they communicated with the spirits through dreaming. The ancient Greeks were very superstitious. In addition to devotion to their gods, they believed in ghosts and portent through the Delphic and other temple oracles, and through dreamtime experiences.[7] The philosopher Plato's adherence to divination and his belief in esoteric worlds reflected this but his pupil, Aristotle, rejected all notions of the supernatural and fortune telling in relation to dreaming.

Aristotle was born in Stagira in 384 BC. When he was about 17, he joined the Academy founded by Plato and remained there until 347. By then, Aristotle had become tutor to Alexander the Great. In addition to the instigation of western thought, Aristotle founded empirical science. He believed it possible to discern the nature of the forces underpinning the natural world through the observation of effects.

He wrote books on many topics, including the earth sciences and in his book, *On Sleep and Wakefulness*, he explains how dreaming is the result of an excited brain. He theorized that the sleeping mind played with material absorbed by the brain during waking hours and returned it to the conscious mind in the form of dream imagery. This all sounds present and correct to us, but it was revolutionary in Aristotle's day.

Aristotle believed that disturbance during sleep, for example, a draught or a faint noise, could trigger off a dream without waking up

---

7   R C T Parker, 'Dreams in Ancient Greece' in *The Oxford Companion to the Mind*, p. 203.

the subject. He believed that, without the judgement of conscious hours, the sleeper accepted uncritically all of his fantastical experiences and that waking up brought that familiar jolt of surprise. Aristotle's theory is not a million miles removed from where our dream theory is now. Considering that he had no access to modern tracking equipment, Aristotle's achievement was stupendous, a true mark of his genius.

Since the time of Aristotle, what we believe about dreams and dreaming has swung wildly between utter rationality, which in our understanding of the term, comes close to meaning what Shakespeare has written, through the voice of Mercutio in *Romeo and Juliet*: "the children of an idle brain, begot of nothing but vain fantasy", 1:4 97-98) and between belief in the literal and symbolic events of the actual dream. In the Bible, dreamers – in both the Old and New Testaments - treated dreams with great respect. In the Old Testament, Joseph, the son of Jacob and the great-grandson of Abraham, was subject to strange dreams that he was able to interpret readily.[8] One day, he told his brothers of a dream he'd had where he and they were binding sheaves in a field. His sheaf stood upright while all of the other sheaves bowed before it.

This angered the brothers since they felt that Joseph was setting himself above them. Here, I digress: in future sections, I spell out the dangers of revealing too much dream information, too soon. From the events in Genesis, it is evident that the young Joseph had not yet attained the wisdom of knowing when to speak out and when to stay silent. In another dream, he saw the sun, moon and eleven stars bowing to him. This dream unsettled Jacob and Rachel, his parents, and incensed his brothers so much that they plotted to kill him. But his eldest brother, Rueben, intervened and instead of killing him, the brothers threw Joseph down a well in the desert. He was "rescued" by merchants on their way to Egypt, but they took him with them and sold him to Potiphar, the

---

8   Book of Genesis, 38: 5-11.

Pharaoh's favourite official, a post that provided him with opportunities to continue his career of interpreting dreams.[9]

Years following Joseph's appointment, the Pharaoh had a very strange dream.[10] He saw seven fat cows on the banks of the Nile being devoured by seven lean cows. He then dreamed of seven healthy ears of grain being devoured by seven meagre ears of grain. Pharaoh summoned all of the wise men and magicians in Egypt but no one was able to tell him the meaning of the dream. But Joseph told Pharaoh that seven years of harvest plenty would be followed by seven years of famine. The only way to prevent disaster, he told Pharaoh, was to build stores of surplus grain during the years of plenty with which to feed the people during the years of want. Pharaoh believed Joseph and immediately appointed him as the official to effectively organise the storing of the grain. By now, Joseph was thirty. In a chariot given him by Pharaoh, he travelled all over Egypt, building granaries and ordering farmers to store one fifth of their harvests. Following seven years of plenty, famine did indeed strike. From all over the known world, people came to buy food from Egyptian stores, thus ensuring its wealth and status as a powerful Mediterranean nation.

Belief in dreams as prophecy held fast, even following the coming of Christianity. Joseph of the New Testament is warned in a dream to take his wife and the child Jesus, and to flee the Holy Land and Herod in favour of Egypt.[11]

Throughout the Middle Ages, growing literacy gave rise to writers and visionaries who made their dreams the focus of poems and stories, a type of writing known as the dream vision, long and elaborate narratives where virtues such as hope and faith are personified as actual people,

---

9   Book of Genesis, 39: 7-20.
10   Book of Genesis, 41: 1-57.
11   Gospel of Matthew, 1:20-24

acting out dramas in which moral lessons are allegorized. Perhaps the most famous tract of all is *The Vision of Piers Plowman* written by William Langland (1332-1400). In this book, the writer attacks what he sees as abuses within the Christian church.[12] But by the sixteenth century, belief in the divine meaning of the dream was waning, a matter which lay behind Mercutio's scornful comment to Romeo. Advances in science meant that Enlightenment was at hand, and by the nineteenth century, disciplines such as neurology had taken its place alongside physiology and psychology.

Born in the seventeenth century, natural philosopher Gottfried Wilhelm Von Leibniz (1646-1716) wrote books on politics, law, ethics, theology, history and philology. He was the first scientist to introduce the idea of the *unconscious*, a full century before the emergence of the disciplines associated with Enlightenment, and *two* centuries before the writings of pre-eminent psychologist, Sigmund Freud.[13] The work of Von Leibniz directly influenced that of Herman Von Helmholtz, who founded the science of *perceptual physiology*.[14] Born in 1821, Helmholz held professorships in various universities, exploring how nervous stimuli – sound, light, touch – sensations are perceived in the brain. Helmholz theorized that these perceptions influenced the unconscious mind as much as the wide-awake conscious mind, all used as fodder for creating the imagery that our subconscious sends us while we are in the REM state – and not at all unlike the theories of Aristotle.

12   Anthony Burgess, *English Literature*
     (Essex: Longman Group, 1974), p. 28.
13   Ralph CS Walker, 'Leibniz, Gottfried, Wilhelm, Frei-Herr von (1646-1716)' in *The Oxford Companion to the Mind*, p. 433.
14   Richard L. Gregory, 'Helmholz, Herrman, Ludwig Ferdinand von (1821-94)' in *The Oxford Companion to the Mind*, p. 308.

HYPNOTISM AND SIGMUND FREUD

In many Hollywood movies, you hear a hypnotherapist say to his patient: *you are now in a deep sleep*. What he actually does is put the patient into a stage between the waking and sleeping state, thus making him or her susceptible to suggestions such as "you are now filled with confidence" or "you will find smoking a cigarette horrible". The theory is that the suggestion sinks into the subconscious of the patient and that he carries the effects of the session into everyday life.

The word "hypnos" is Greek in origin, derived from Hypnus, the mythological personification of sleep, with Somnus being the Roman equivalent. This etymology has given rise to interesting word variants. When you are falling asleep, your brain is in a hypnogogic state and when you are emerging from dreaming sleep into wakefulness, your brain is in a hypnopompic state. In the hypnogogic state, your brain is highly open to suggestion, which is the basis of hypnosis. And "Somnus" is the basis of "somnambulism", the clinical word for sleepwalking, a sleep disorder that I describe in the section **Sleep Disorders and Nightmares**.

It was the lateral thinking of psychoanalyst Sigmund Freud that opened the way for the therapeutic interpretation of dreams. Freud's therapy involved hypnotising a patient until he or she could talk openly about everything, including intimate matters that were taboo in repressive, late nineteenth-century Vienna. He reasoned that if the intimate musings of a patient were symptomatic of his or her state of mind, the same must apply to the dream imagery that stemmed from the patient's unconscious. This pathology is equivalent to blood analysis for detecting physical disease.

Sigmund Freud (1856-1939) was an Austrian neurologist who founded the practice of *psychoanalysis*, a method of treating mental disorders. In tandem with his colleague, Josef Breuer, Freud developed a technique known as *free association*, a method of training the mind to gain access to the unconscious process.[15] The material in this book will enable the reader to discern the parallel between free association and Aristotle's theory of the dreaming process, that is, the ability of the unconscious mind to withdraw the judgement of the conscious hours, so that the sleeper can uncritically accept all manner of fantastical experiences.

In the longer term, Freud developed his own set of theories about dreaming, including that of wish-fulfilment, and in 1900, six years following the death of Helmholtz, he published his findings in *The Interpretation of Dreams*. Freud believed that the material that rose from the unconscious during sleep was symbolical of the repressed desires of patients – as he called his subjects – and that dreaming about a desire could fulfil it. However, I have always been uncomfortable with this hypotheses of Freud. I fail to understand of how merely dreaming of a desire can fulfil it; quite the opposite, in fact. And I disagree with his theory that all of our desires spring from the longing to fulfil the most basic of our needs, food and shelter, survival and sex. I believe that much dreaming involves our need for the "higher" things in life, the desire to experience culture, music, the arts and literature – and the need of certain subjects to create and invent. However, while Freud was a practising psychologist, he met a promising young student.

Carl Jung (1875-1961) had considered a number of careers before becoming a doctor. He entered the University of Basel in 1895 to study medicine.[16] Years later, his colleague Eugen Bleuler, whom he met in the Burgholzi psychiatric hospital in Zurich, introduced him to Freud. Initially, the two psychologists were in friendly, professional collaboration, but their theories began to diverge. Jung had travelled

15   David Angus Graham Cook, 'Free Association' in *The Oxford Companion*, p. 266.
16   DAG Cook, 'Jung, Carl Gustav (1875-1961)' in *The Oxford Companion*, pp. 404-406.

much and established cultural similarities between subjects dreaming in similar geographical locations.

Unlike Freud, he did not believe that dreams stemmed from repressed desires, but that dream images stemmed from the *collective unconscious*, that store of collective ancestral dreams and memories common to all cultures.[17] In addition, Jung believed that the meaning of symbols in a dream differed according to the culture in which the subject had emerged from, the age of the dreamer, his state of health and other social circumstances. Another dimension that Jung added to psychoanalysis is *individuation*, that is, healing the person by balancing the personality by developing underdeveloped traits.[18] Jung's process of individuation was concerned with bringing the unconscious into the conscious for the better functioning of the self. Freud believed that what we call the "self" was a conglomerate of desires, both rational and irrational, that sprang from the ego, the *entitled* part of self. By contrast, Jung believed that the ego was just a unit in a tripartite construction of self that also consisted of the *conscious* and *unconscious*. Jung believed that the ego is merely the facet of self that we reveal to others, and its healthy functioning depends upon communication between the conscious and the unconscious. The better the communication, the healthier the person and the personality.

For much of his life, Jung travelled and lectured, forming friendships with priests and shamans. He recognised that particular tropes, that is, figures of speech and modes of thought, were common to certain cultures. For instance, why in the west, do many people describe a ghost they might have seen as a "grey lady"? The UFO phenomenon that erupted during the 1950s captured his attention and made him wonder

---

17 DAG Cook, 'Jung, Carl Gustav (1875-1961)' in *The Oxford Companion*, p. 404.
18 DAG Cook, 'Jung, Carl Gustav (1875-1961)' in *The Oxford Companion*, p. 404.

about *flying saucers* and *little green men* – and more about those in a further chapter. Jung died in 1961.

Jung is the psychologist that I am most in accord with because he recognized that human needs have evolved beyond those of the animals and the most basic of desires. No other species on Earth embraces cultural activity and religion, mythology and folklore as humans do, the reason that dream images are often cultural tropes in disguise. Like Jung, I believe that the majority of people who wish to explore their personalities beneath a superficial level are not ill, but seeking completeness. However, I admire Freud, as Carl Jung undoubtedly did, as the father of modern psychology, and the first person to actually lay down a theory of dreams. He wrote and spoke about sex in a society where the subject was all but forbidden. But in accordance with Jung, I do not believe you can separate the mentality of the *majority* of people from the society in which we live and work.

DREAMS AND GESTALT

Even while Freud and Jung were at work, other theories of psychoanalysis were emerging. During the 1890's, the Berlin School of Experimental Psychology became the centre for the practice of Gestalt or Gestaltism, its chief advocate being psychologist Kurt Koffka.[19] His quotation: "the whole is other than the sum of its parts" has gone into history. Put simply, our conscious brains have a tendency to "compensate" for what we think is missing from a series of images or sounds. No doubt you have already mentally placed a square - which I

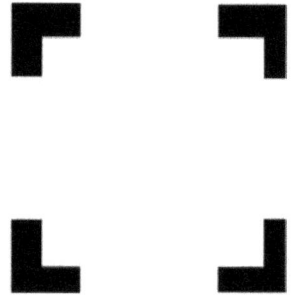

---

19   'Koffka, Kurt (1886-1941)' in *The Oxford Companion*, p. 412.

did not draw - into the image above. And without realising that we are doing it, we have all "finished" the verse of a snatch of a popular song heard on someone's radio in a passing car.

Graphic designers and advertising executives use this phenomenon to great effect, nudging our brains into recognising brand names and associating consumables with our favourite sounds from the hit parade. However, in the real world, constant mental compensation can lead to a deficit of true knowledge, to misperception and ultimately damaging misunderstanding. We see this sometimes in highly publicised court cases where a series of witnesses, the majority totally honest, offer a slightly different version of the same incident. The jury then has the unenviable task of unravelling the testimonies and deciding what really happened. Incidentally, the jury "going out" process is analogous to what happens in our brains while we sleep.

The objects, events and people we see as dream imagery is our subconscious building a total picture of what is really happening in our lives. Unlike an advertising executive trying to appeal to the masses, your subconscious is talking directly to you, hinting at the deficits in your actions. In a similar way, Gestalt therapists bring their patients through various exercises, helping them to see the total picture of a situation or even their own personalities. In the chapter, **Meditative Exercises**, my section on Gestalt includes a short exercise on how to draw further information from dreams. However, although I refer to various methodologies now and again throughout the text, be aware that in no way do I favour one method of dream interpretation over any other. At this point, I will explain a little about levels of awareness or consciousness, and why an understanding of this subject is helpful when approaching dream theory.

Levels of awareness
and dream perception

TWO ILLUMINATING STATES OF MIND

The easiest way to explain states of awareness is to look at how they operate in our waking hours. It's like this. You are engrossed in a task, one that is of vital importance to you. It could be that you are revising for an important exam. You might be cleaning your house in preparation for an extra special guest or preparing an assignment to meet a very stringent work deadline. Whatever it is, you are giving yourself totally and utterly to the task; no feature is overlooked and no detail is too mundane to attend to. Whatever happens, you have got to get it right.

During your task, you need to get a glass of water. As you leave your station, you happen to glance out of the window and you find that the sky has turned bright pink. No it's not April 1 or approaching dawn. It is the middle of the day and the sun has been shining in a bright blue sky all morning. With a sense of irritation, you take your drink and go back to your station. Is it pollution or a practical joke, you wonder, and if it *is* a joke, have people nothing better to do? Maybe not, but you have your task to complete and so you get on with it. Apart from this vague sense of annoyance, you are unruffled.

Now, think of another scenario. You are sitting indoors, looking out the window, with nothing particular to do. As in the earlier scenario, you see the sky turning pink. There is no question that you have fallen asleep and are dreaming; you *know* that you are wide awake. Astonishment turns to alarm, which turns to fear. Are aliens attacking the earth or is something desperately wrong with your eyesight? You go outside and find the nearest police station, which is thronged with people as frightened as you are, while the powers-that-be alert the military. Both the scenarios describe the same event, filtered through two levels of consciousness. In the first, you are so engrossed in a personal task that not even a pink sky can disrupt the process. In the second, you are so open to suggestion that the sight of a pink sky fills your mind with all kinds of alarming theories. With nothing to do, you are close to the *hypnagogic* (falling sleep from wakefulness) or *hypnopompic* (waking from sleep) state and extremely open to suggestion, thus your alarm at the pink sky.

WHICH STATE IS THE "RIGHT" ONE?

With reference to these levels of consciousness, let me stress here that neither state is "superior" to the other. Though the first state might seem the more rational, it could be that you come to regret the fun that you have missed by *not* dashing outside and witnessing the general excitement. This second state might have prompted you to write a best-selling book about the day the sky turned pink. The point is, the scenarios chart one mind in two states of awareness, both essential for mental health. Before I move into the depths of brain theory, I want to explain a little about the subconscious.

THE MARVELLOUS SUBCONSCIOUS

The world "sub" literally means "underneath", something that is there but that is hidden from view. Curiously, the better parts of us remain hidden from view, throughout our lives – just think of the cranial activity that goes on underneath our rather superficial scalps? Or think of the power of the Internet, that marvellous worldwide transmission network that might be bringing home the very words that you are reading now. Computers and smartphones may be glamorous items but they are merely superficial interfaces that enable us to connect with a universe of information.

To use another allegory: most people have in their homes a kind of store, an attic or cellar, filled with things put by for occasional use. These are usually toolboxes, long-read books, Christmas decorations, garden furniture for use in summer, skis for winter, and so on. In many homes, the same store is used to conceal items for which there is no obvious use but that the owner can't let go of; stashes of paid-up bills and financial statements, albums filled with keepsake photographs and clothes that may be old and worn, but are still treasured. Whether in the attic or not, we all have stores of such items. Our subconscious serves the same function, a repository of dreams and memories that we push into the "store", since keeping them constantly in our conscious brain will only weigh heavily and slow down our immediate mode of thinking. When we dream, we draw upon this repository of memories and impressions to construct the archetypes that act out our nocturnal dramas. Just as a total stranger can look into your closet and build a credible biography from the possessions that are important to you, continual scrutiny of your archetypes can reveal your state of mind – to you. And it is this state that underlies your beliefs about and attitudes to everything, beliefs that will carry you far, if you allow them. Useful as this allegory is, it is not exact; exploring your closet won't reveal your future, but getting acquainted with your subconscious can have a profound impact upon it – and this is the chief purpose of dreaming. But why?

THE SPLIT BRAIN

Our brains consist of two halves, with the right side of the brain controlling the left side of the body and vice versa, linked together by a rope-like bundle of nerves known as the *corpus callum*. In their book, *The Awakened Mind*, C Maxwell Cade and Nona Coxhead explain how areas of the left brain control logical functions, which overall means the ability to draw conclusions based on one thing following another, examples being a maths theorem or a laid-out argument. Logical function covers verbal skills, sequencing, counting, analysing and reasoning.[20]

In her best-selling book, *Drawing on the Right Side of the Brain*, author and artist, Betty Edwards demonstrates how the majority of people are over reliant on the left side of the brain, thus cutting themselves off from sources of information and creative expression offered by the right side of the brain. Logical and numerical skills may serve the jobs' market well, but over-dependence on using these may result in imbalance in our lives and personalities. The right half of the brain controls non-verbal function, that is, an awareness of things without the necessity of linking them to words. Since the majority of us are right-handed, the left half of the brain predominates everything we do. But it is here that creativity begins, imagination, hunches and intuition, those things that we know without being able to say (in words) why. And it is here that dream imagery comes from since most of the time we dream in pictures. The next question is: how do we get both sides of the brain to work in harmony?

Here, I introduce writer Colin Wilson, prolific author of fiction and philosophy. In an essay entitled 'Fantasy and Faculty X', Wilson explains that science has established that the brain halves work at different speeds, with the left half generally working more quickly than the right.[21] Wilson theorized that we are at our most creative when our two brain halves are working in harmony, that is, at the same speed.

---

20 Maxwell & Coxhead, *The Awakened Mind:* pp. 49-52.
21 Colin Wilson 'Fantasy and Faculty X' in Williamson, JN (ed.), *How to Write Tales of Horror, Fantasy & Science Fiction* (London: Robinson Publishing, 1990), p. 134.

When we are asleep or even relaxing, the right half of the brain takes over from the left half, sending imagery from our subconscious, the part of our consciousness that is between waking and sleeping, to cognitive sites like memory. We forget most of this imagery on awakening, but the dreams we do remember are most often coded information from the most creative part of the brain. In contrast to the left brain, the right brain is adept at *synthesis* and it is this synthetic function of the brain that brings dream imagery together in a way that can help us build a more holistic model of our personal environments. Once again, I stress that this book is not a manual on how to transform into a mystic or a guru. My aim is to help the reader attain more ready access to the creative state, through exercises that I lay out further on in the book.

THE DANGER OF ABSTRACTIONS

One matter that our conscious brain excels at is seizing upon a detail and abstracting it, that is, making it stand for something other or greater than it is. Because we are so good at this, we have come to consider entire rafts of abstractions as constituting the "whole picture". Recognising abstractions brings great benefits, of course. Urban planning experts draw upon the abstracting faculty all the time in designing traffic systems and placing recognizable signs so that motorists and pedestrians will know where to walk and where to drive, when to stop and when to go. In fact, an entire meta-language of signs and symbols now occupies our town and city centres, signs that indicate where to find shops and restaurants, transport links and public bathrooms.

Where coordinated behaviour is essential for safety and even survival, this is a good thing. However, it would greatly diminish the quality of our lives if we relied *only* upon these signs for information, ignoring other clues and definite indicators of what is taking place in the environment. Just imagine going through life without noticing the store fronts and human population, the street performers and vendors, or hearing music and seeing colour, and all the other variables that go into defining rich, urban environments?

Our personal lives are riddled with abstractions of all kinds, conundrums that most often we do not have time to pause and unravel. However, failing to build a total picture of signs and abstractions can have unfortunate, even fatal consequences – think of ignoring health symptoms, or indications of a relationship or a career in trouble? The mother shouting angrily at her toddler is not necessarily *angry with him*; more likely, she is trying to save him from danger, a hot stove, moving traffic, whatever. The person *running* is as likely to be running *towards* (a loved one, a bus stop?) as *away* from something (a fire, pursuit by the law?)

Consider the use of sat-nav devices in cars, which can be very useful. You are uncertain of the way to a destination, so you employ a device that has reduced the journey to a series of right-turn, left turn operations, directions laid down by a subject who has already made the journey. Used with caution, these devices can save you from much frustration, in terms of time, in getting to your destination. But too many incidents (see **Appendix B**), a number of them tragic, highlight the dangers of slavishly following reductive directions.

It is because of this deficit in the hours of *consciousness* that the *unconscious* takes over while we sleep, putting us in touch with the *subconscious*, which is why dreaming is vital for mental health. And this is why I stress again and again the importance of harvesting and analysing as much dream material as possible, to take into account fleeting oneiric or dream-time events concerning a subject or two, or simply you and much intense emotion, in addition to those big dreams so filled with people and events that you wake up feeling as if you have been in another place or time?

THE BRAIN AND AWARENESS

Above, I have subjectively described two states of awareness. Throughout the twentieth century, various specialist writers, psychologists and philosophers, including PD Ouspensky and John C. Lilly, defined levels of consciousness according to the subjectively-described states of mind of various persons. In their book, Cade and Coxhead describe their use of EEG and other electronic equipment to track the levels of brain activity of subjects – students of brain monitoring science, patients and practitioners – in various states of consciousness, sleeping, waking and meditation.[22] From their findings, the authors created a table outlining a hierarchy of mental states, in which they show the various brainwaves detected by their equipment throughout their experiments, alpha *(calm, detached awareness)* beta *(problem solving awareness)*, theta *(hypnagogic or half-awake state)* and so forth. From their findings, they compiled a table in which they charted the various levels of awareness experienced by both waking and sleeping subjects. State 1 is deep sleep (NREM) and state 2 is hypnagogic (moving into sleep from wakefulness) and hypnopompic (waking up after sleep), both REM states. State 3 is that impaired awareness that the majority of us experience after just having woken up. State 4 is normal wakeful awareness and state 5 is lucid awareness, while State 6 is the level at which we attain heightened levels of creativity. This state, I quote: "provides the opportunity for us to avail ourselves of our hitherto unmanifested creativity by transmitting of dreamlike imagery from the right to the left hemisphere of the brain". [23]

In summary, it is possible, while awake, to attain a state of mind that enables the subject to directly access the level of consciousness that sends dream imagery to the conscious brain. I have already explained how Colin Wilson theorized that great creative works were born when

22   Cade and Coxhead, *The Awakened Mind*, p. 43.
23   Cade and Coxhead, *The Awakened Mind*, p. 85

the two brain halves worked in harmony. Either the left half slowed its pace so that it could receive information from the right – or the right half speeded its pace so that it fell in step with the left. Since the latter process normally happens when the subject is under the influence of stimulants, alcohol and other, possibly harmful substances, I do not advocate this course of action to the reader. Not only do I lean towards the slower process of *dream analysis* combined with *meditative* techniques, I find it fascinating that Wilson's Faculty X is actually a description of how dream images pop into consciousness just as you are drifting asleep or waking up. Interestingly, Wilson expresses again and again that Faculty X is the state of "super-consciousness", in which the subject experiences a kind of heightened reality as the kind of consciousness that inspires artists, writers and other creative people. The wider point is that these states of awareness do exist objectively, and that everyone has the potential to reach all of them *without the use of narcotics*, even Faculty X.

We experience "normal" awareness, and dreaming and dreamless sleep without even trying to. When a task calls for extra concentration, the majority of us have learned how to focus, and to get to the nitty-gritty and do whatever it takes. However, this frame of mind is quite distinct from those dreamy, floaty feelings of suggestibility. No one would expect enhanced performance from a half-awake or half-asleep subject, though some people try to force this, usually with unfortunate results. And the majority of us know how difficult it is for a brain weighed by worry and grief to focus upon anything at all. We need bouts of lucidity to complete complex tasks, just as we need intervals of the hypnagogic/hypnopompic state to stay in touch with the imagery sent us by our subconscious. The exercises in this book will guide you through processes that draw creativity from both states of mind, plus meditative exercises that may help you attain super-consciousness. But why does paying attention to dream imagery help with everyday life, whether you are simply trying to live a life, free from strife, or working on creative tasks?

Dreams and Achievement

SHAKESPEARE ON DREAMING

In this chapter, I take a closer look at that statement of William Shakespeare: "dreams, /Which are the children of an idle brain." Shakespeare was writing his plays when the world was moving out of medieval superstition and into a more rational, scientific age. On the cusp of this new world, the Bard was making the case for *not* interpreting a dream as a religious visitation or a portent, but simply recognising dream imagery as a type of mental detritus, rising to consciousness following an eventful day or week. And indeed, this hypothesis has much to commend it. But let us look at that phrase once more:

"the children of an idle brain"

Supposing we substitute the word "idle" with "resting"? And then, we replace "children" with "chatter"? Rephrased, we could write the sentence:

"dreams, the chatter of a resting brain".

In other words, when your brain *rests*, it *chatters* back to you with matters that affect you daily, playing back to you events and emotions that you have not had the time or inclination to dwell upon throughout waking consciousness, most likely because everyday tasks and duties stand between you and a deeper understanding of your situation. Most often, these details are disguised as symbols and archetypes – more about these later on – because the information sent by your subconscious is valuable. It is meant for you and you alone to interpret. I believe that when the Bard provided this description of the dreaming mind, he was not deprecating the information that we receive from our subconscious while we sleep or rest; he was merely couching the difference between the wakeful and sleeping consciousness in poetic terminology. After all, no one would deny the value of *children*, now would they? And I believe that the Bard himself had access to a store of creativity unavailable to the undeveloped mind; from where else did he draw delectable word images such as:

> "she hangs upon the cheek of night/ As a rich jewel in an Ethiop's ear" (*Romeo and Juliet*, 1:5:43-44)

and:

> "I love! I sue! I seek a wife!/A woman, that is like a
> German clock,
> Still a-repairing, ever out of frame,/And never going aright, being a watch,
> But being watch'd that it may still go right!
> (*Love's Labour's Lost*, 3:1:179-183)

and:

> "Look how the floor of heaven/ Is thick inlaid with patines of bright gold:
> There's not the smallest orb which thou behold'st /But in his motion like an angel sings, /Still quiring to the young-eyed cherubins" (*Merchant of Venice*, 5:1:58-62)

And there are many more. And I find it difficult to believe that Shakespeare and other Renaissance geniuses, such as Leonardo da Vinci and Michelangelo Buonarotti, had *not* a hot line to their subconscious, had *not* found a direct way to draw upon the stream of creativity that is available to everyone who learns how to use it.

Whether or not these worthy subjects drew upon the power of dreams to aid and abet their creativity is a moot point. But the fact is, they were all creative powerhouses, and their powers came from "somewhere" and that somewhere just *may* have been the world of dreams. And this power is available to you, and you can learn to use it too. But back to Shakespeare's words: my belief is that this quotation stemmed from his positivity about the power of dreaming, not otherwise.

Put less poetically: dreams behave almost like chattering people in a public house, mulling over the day's events when the sun has gone down – and who would denigrate the importance of listening to "ordinary" people talking among one another, listening to and understanding their concerns, fears and hopes and possibly, solutions to their problems? Many a politician has won an election doing as much, I am sure. And this allegory stresses the importance of recording all dreams, no matter how insignificant they may seem, not just the very vivid and memorable ones – a matter that I stress, throughout the text.

WHAT'S THE BIG IDEA?

For years, I dreamed about dreaming up a great business idea - or the words of a hit song - or the plot of a best-selling book, followed by my waking up and jumping out of bed, of my getting down to brass tacks and making my name and my fortune – and this has happened to a number of people. The creative world is awash with tales of artists who have dreamed and turned their downtime phantasms into daytime reality and I did not see why I should not be one of them. Paul McCartney reputedly dreamed the lyrics of the hit song, *Yesterday*. Elias Howe found the solution to perfecting his invention, the sewing machine, when he dreamed of a fierce, spear-throwing tribe – and the spears all had holes close to the arrowheads. The world of chemistry still charts how Friedrich Kekule's dream enabled him to establish the structure of the benzene molecule. For years, he and other chemists had puzzled over it and

Kekule solved the mystery when he realised that the molecule might be circular rather than linear. However, Howe, McCartney, and Kekule already had gained much in terms of fame, expertise and sheer determination, when their inspiration arrived. They were grafters who had travelled much upon their individual paths and were not going to lie down on their journeys. Otherwise, those dreams of snakes, spears and snatches of poetry would have gotten flipped away with a change of bedlinen.

This is why I urge all you dreamers to begin keeping a dream diary, and to constantly evaluate and work to make use of the ideas they contain. The sewing machine has long been with us and the structure of the benzene molecule is universal, but somewhere in your notes might be lurking an idea or combo of them that will put you on the path to fame and gain. That is why I now introduce the concept of analogical thinking.

CONCRETE THINKING AND DREAMING

Analogical thinking is all around us. Fizzy pop bursting from a glass bottle can demonstrate the workings of a volcano. Tying a tennis ball to a post and pulling or batting it around can help explain the principle of gravity, while Albert Einstein formulated his theory of relativity by imagining himself sitting on a beam of light and travelling through the universe. It is more than 30 years since *A Whack on the Side of the Head: How you can be more creative*, by Roger Von Oech became a runaway bestseller. It still sells, and Von Oech has produced a number of knock-on follow-ups, such as *A Kick in the Seat of the Pants* (1996) and *Expect the Unexpected, or You Won't Find It* (2001). The 1983 book does what it says on the cover, offering readers a blow-by-blow set of techniques on how to transform everyday situations into creative and, if appropriate, financial capital. And yes, Von Oech does include a section "Listen to

Your Dreams", endorsing everything I have already discovered about night-time imagery – thank you, Roger.[24]

In his broader discourse on creativity, Von Oech advocates analogical thinking, that is, the creation of *equivalences* between what, on the surface, are very different situations in order to arrive at practical solutions to problems. We see this when scientists run rodents through hoops and hurdles so they can see what humans might behave like in similar situations...hmmm!

And above all, Von Oech advocates *taking action*, in tandem with all of the great and wonderful creative ideas that his exercises in creativity conjure up. And his ideas have inspired me to create my nine-point outline to action:

First, in order to achieve anything, you are bound to be dissatisfied with life as it is. Life might be good, but you want it quite a bit better – else why do you experience all of those dreams from which you awaken, filled with longing and that feeling that you have not fulfilled your destiny? You may be longing for a lover to share your good fortune with, you may want a promotion at work – or you may be in search of an entirely new career?

Second, make a map of where you want to go. Using a computer graphics' package, place a photograph of yourself as you are now at a "start" banner and a photo of what you want to achieve at a "finish" banner. The end point could be a beautiful new house, a handsome or lovely "other half", or an image of a faraway destination that you have always dreamed of going to. Or you could graft the image of an academic mortarboard on to your own portrait. Then, place other banners about

---

24   Von Oech, Roger, *A Whack on the Side of the Head: How you can be More Creative* (Wellingborough: Thorsons Publishers Limited), pp. 128-130.

the board, tagged with the obstacles you might encounter; lack of money, qualifications, social contacts and so on.

Third, for every obstacle banner, create a solution label. For instance, against "lack of money" write, "work overtime" or "sell old DVDs" or "take extra job" – whatever steps are available to you. For "lack of qualifications" write "more study" – perhaps you can persuade an employer to sponsor a college course?

Fourth, place a time limit on your achievement. The majority of people "make it" while they are still young and although existentially, achievement has no time limit, learning to be economical in this area will help you engender ideas more quickly – and make way for even greater achievement!

Fifth, before you begin, decide what is at stake. Imagine yourself in five or ten years' time, alone and unloved, or doing the same job that you are doing now, or simply living in the same house and with the same set of acquaintances, ones that you have long outgrown. Unless you are *really happy* with where you are now – in which case you would not be reading this – it is not an attractive picture.

Sixth: find a support system. Tell a carefully chosen friend about your plans and charge him or her with ensuring that you see them through. And this is not a one-way street; you can serve the same purpose when your friend requires help.

Seventh, be courageous; faint heart never won fair lady. It isn't easy pushing yourself forward in order to achieve something exceptional, but you will never know until you try – and think how you will feel if you *don't* try?

Eighth, if the orthodox ways of gaining momentum do not work for you, conjure new and unusual ways of "selling" your ideas; exploring your dream material will help you here. When I was trying to find an outlet for my online literary courses, a dream about standing in front of an audience led to my creation of my literary lectures. If you have no success with the available range of dating agencies, perhaps you can begin your own agency? If you really can't afford to study, perhaps you can persuade an employer to sponsor a college course?

Ninth, whatever you do, persist in your endeavour. In addition to persistence being a tenet of all achievement, the more engaged you are with your plans, the more that you impress upon your subconscious that you intend to succeed, and the more dream material you will receive. And in one or more dreams, you may find the "missing link", the idea or combination of ideas that will provide the route to your achievement.

Least you still have doubts about the benefits of dream-gathering, just consult *Dreaming for Success* (978-1467923156), by Dr Carl Patrasso, a clinical psychologist who has been writing about dreams and dreaming for many years. The book is a compendium of the potential power of using dreams for success in every area of life, including relationships, work and good health. Before I move forward with the practical information in this book, I want to explain in a little more detail how the collective dreams of generations have provided a path to the mental maturity of countless millions of people.

The Fairy Tale:
Literature and Art

"Considering the important role such unconscious desires, needs, pressures, and anxieties play in behaviour, new insights into oneself from dreams permit a person to arrange his life much more successfully".[25]

Bruno Bettelheim was born in Austria in 1903. A student of Freudian psychology, he trained as a doctor and specialised in treating childhood disorders and disturbances. Throughout his distinguished international career, he published many books, including *The Uses of Enchantment: The Meaning and Importance of Fairy Tales*, which he produced in 1976. In the book, Bettelheim argues against the fashionable view of *not* telling traditional fairy tales to young children. He explains how the stock fairytale figures, such as princes and princesses, wicked stepmothers, giants and witches, are all symbols that embody the hopes and fears of the very young. He expresses again and again that the fables are not meant to be taken literally, but that they enable their young listeners to engage with and express their fears and desires vicariously, and thus promote emotional growth.

Writes Bettelheim "The child who is familiar with fairy tales understands that these speak to him in the language of symbols and not that of everyday reality."[26] And the reason that children need fairy tales

---

25 Bettelheim, *The Uses of Enchantment*, p.54
26 Bettelheim, *The Uses of Enchantment*, p. 62.

is because few of them have the emotional maturity to deal with the "adult" symbols that appear in the dreams of older people. The writer Charlotte Bronte presaged this view over one century earlier when she wrote, through the voice of her most famous character, Jane Eyre: "Children can feel but they cannot analyze their feelings; and if the analysis is partially effected in thought, they know not how to express the result of the process in words".[27] Early in the Bronte narrative, we see a bruised and battered (mentally) Jane asking her friend Bessie for her favourite book, *Gulliver's Travels*, in which she reads about fantastical places such as Lilliput and Brobdignag.[28]

Essentially, fairy tales behave like old friends and companions, accompanying us on our journeys from youth to maturity. And like the voices of wise adults, they tell us the same truths over and over again, in ways that are palatable and digestible to the young mind. After all, what child wants to listen constantly to a nagging adult?

Little Red Riding Hood translates easily into a fable on taking care while out of doors, while other tales are disguised parables on the values of honesty, constancy and earnest labour. More subtle and more difficult to decipher are the stock endings of the traditional tales that seem to contravene all modern values of social and gender equality, endings that have caused howls of derision in our times. To take one stock fairytale ending "the prince and princess got married and lived happily ever after". Bettelheim points out that the true meaning of such an ending is a reconciliation of the contradictory elements within ourselves rather than a desire for personal aggrandizement. We are all unique, our personalities a blend of elements that are quite often in conflict and seemingly, to the *conscious* subject, irreconcilable.

27 Bronte, Charlotte, *Jane Eyre*, ed. Margaret Smith (Oxford: Oxford University Press), p. 40.
28 Bronte, *Jane Eyre*, p. 21.

However, maturity arrives when the subject learns to control these disparate and apparently contradictory elements that make us who we are, for example, "male" and "female". We all have traits of both genders in our personalities, and the statement that *the prince and princess live happily together* is not paving the way for little girls to desperately want pink net gowns and glittery tiaras, or for young boys to get involved in knife crime. It is a disguised way of saying that the *balanced* subject of either gender will learn to live in harmony with himself or herself, and others. I was so struck by this wonderful book that I analysed the story of *Aladdin and his Magic Lamp* according to the Bettelheim methodologies.

The results astonished me; *Aladdin* is not the story I thought it was, and I have reproduced my resulting essay in the **Appendix A**, at the end of this book. The fairy tale is the most wonderful device in which young children can enact their emotional conundrums – but Bettelheim explains all of this much better than I can – do read his wonderful book.

By the time we reach adulthood, the majority of us have gained a modicum of skill in analysing and expressing feelings, a skill that requires a lifetime's practice. Be aware that adults never really and truly stop growing emotionally. We, too, need to grapple with fears and desires and when we have finished reading "childish" fairy tales, dream analysis is an appropriate medium by which to do this. And Bettelheim endorses dream analysis for adults, even though it might exact a personal cost: "With Freud's influence, our dreams have become much more problematic to us – more upsetting and difficult to deal with. But they are also a royal road to the unconscious mind, and they permit us to form a new and richer view of ourselves, and our humanity."[29] Throughout his book, Bettelheim refers to the "dream-like" details in fairy tales; the grotesque, the absurd and the downright impossible

29   Bettelheim, The *Uses of Enchantment*, p. 273

happenings. As with fairytale elements, dream images are not concerned so much with "reality" as with repackaging our fears and aspirations and presenting them to us in a way that we can confront, engage with and if necessary, conquer: "Independence and transcending childhood require personality development, not becoming better at a particular task, or doing battle with external difficulties."[30] And I concur with Bettelheim in believing that the subject who is permitted to vicariously slay dragons and win eternal love, over and over, whether in dreams or in fantasy fiction, is less likely to retreat into the dangerous and intractable fantasy that plagues many adults; drug addiction, involvement with cults, and others.[31] My chapter, **Dream Archetypes**, provides much information on identifying personal archetypes and of how to make use of them.

DREAMS AND OTHER LITERATURE

About one hundred and fifty years ago, Charles Lutwidge Dodgson, under the name of Lewis Carroll, published *Alice's Adventures Under Ground*, which later became *Alice in Wonderland*. I have never read this book without a sense of awe at how a "logical" Oxford mathematician wrote this extraordinary story, filled with strange and magical characters. It is all at once funny, creepy, philosophical - and just plain daft. Because it works on so many levels, several writers have parodied the book or used it as a creative springboard for other works, like stage plays, musicals and movies. These effects aside, I marvel again and again over how a person unknown as a children's author could have entered into such uninhibited wordplay – or maybe I have answered my own question? It is likely that Dodgson derived the character of the Dodo from his own name, which he'd mispronounced because of his stammer, a prime

---

30   Bettelheim, *Uses of Enchantment*, p. 142.
31   Bettelheim, *Uses of Enchantment*, pp. 50-51.

example of wordplay channelled into dream imagery. It would be tiresome and not very helpful to explore every example of "everyday" imagery channelled into the story. What I find most remarkable is that *Alice* predates Surrealism, by approximately fifty years, a cultural movement in which dreams and dreaming provide a pivot for creativity.

DREAMS AND POETRY

If you have ever wondered on reading Samuel T. Coleridge's poem, *Kubla Khan*, why the poet ended the narrative so abruptly, following: "For he on honey-dew hath fed, And drunk the milk of Paradise", take warning from the following tale. The events of the poem came to Coleridge in a dream, which he proceeded to write out, upon awakening. Presently, a tap on the window interrupted him, and he paused in his writing to attend to the "person from Porlock". Later on, Coleridge found that his inspiration had vanished, along with his intruding visitor, and losing forever – *our* loss – a sizeable portion of what may have become one of the greatest epic poems ever?

In a later section, I stress the importance of dream capture. However, a more profound link between the poem and the dream exists, namely the process of establishing archetypes, which is the "backways" process of actually writing a poem. In a typical poetry creation class, students are asked to focus upon one word or idea before building the streams of ideas that presently turn into poems. This technique is available to the lay person, who can make use of it consciously or unconsciously to turn words into concrete works. For many years, I did this without realising what I was doing, for example, gazing at the evening star and making note of the words that drifted into my head: *orb, majesty, shimmering, brilliance, dusky, Earth, blanket, houses, pink, fiery, western* – eventually, I produced the following immortal (sic) lines:

From a blue sky tinged with western fire
The evening star looks down upon a pink-tinted Earth

Fulgent, shimmering in the great beyond
Proud over this hushy, dusky blanket of ground
In vain do our house lights seek to rival her brilliance
Feeble tinsel glints against the majesty of gold
What secrets does she harbour? I wonder
As I gaze awe-struck at the glittering orb;
What ancient sagas has she beheld upon this,
Her companion planet? Slyly, she winks
Revealing only her fabulous light
And bids us Earth dwellers "good night".

Sure, I am a lousy poet, but bear in mind that the idea-gathering phase of interpreting a dream works in much the same way as the word-gathering phase of its analysis.

DREAMS, ART AND IMAGINATION

"Imagination abandoned by Reason produces Monsters; united with her, she is the mother of the arts."

The above words were written, over two hundred years ago, not by a writer but by an artist. In his lifetime, Francisco de Goya (1746-1828) was artist to two Spanish kings, Charles III and Charles IV. In the earlier decades of his career, Goya had created official portraits and representations of the Bourbon monarchs and their families. But with his employment under the progressive and enlightened Charles III having given way, upon the monarch's death to a similar post with his son, the retrogressive and ill-tempered Charles IV, Goya took the opportunity to observe the growing backwardness of the country in which he lived. Ignorance and superstition abounded in a country in which the Spanish Inquisition largely ruled. This political environment was in contrast to the remainder of Europe, which was progressing through the scientific, technological and political upheaval that we now call Enlightenment.

Goya's response was to publish anonymously the *Caprichos*, a set of cartoons or drawings that satirised the country's political situation. As an employee of the crown, Goya could not reveal himself as the artist at the time. In the two hundred years since then, a drawing called *The Sleep of Reason Produces Monsters* has become the most famous of the *Caprichos*. In it, we see a man, his face hidden as he sleeps upon a table. Despite the title, there are no monsters visible but recognisable creatures like bats, owls and a large cat. Many writers have tried to interpret the meaning of the creatures. Art critic William Vaughan suggests a connection with Greek mythology, the owl possibly a symbol of Athena, goddess of wisdom.

Actually, our reason does "sleep" while we dream and unleashes the creative imagery of dreams. When we combine this gift with imagination to produce a work (art, music, literature?) then an artist is born. The full story of the *Caprichos* is too lengthy to reproduce here; however, it is fascinating and do read about it when you can. In 1819, Goya retired from court life. Alone and totally deaf because of illness, he created the *Disparates,* another set of drawings and another story. The nineteenth century had just begun – as had the link between art and dreams.

SURREALISM IN DREAMS

In 1846, a French poet, Isidore-Lucien Ducasse, later known as Comte de Lautréamont, was born. His work, *Les Chants des Maldoror*, was about a character with what we could call alternative views upon the world. Ducasse died in 1870. By the 1920s, the surrealists were creating works of art and poetry. In one of his works, the artist Man Ray referred to a line in a canto of the poem, *Les Chants de Maldoror*: "beautiful as the chance meeting on a dissecting-table of a sewing-machine and an umbrella", a word image that provokes that familiar, queasy sensation as experienced in a dream when we encounter an unusual, unlikely or even unsettling juxtaposition of people and events, for example, seeing our best friend's mum in a compromising situation with another person's male relative. And the realisation that the image is just a construct parallels the relief upon awakening from an unpleasant dream. In the wake of Andre Breton publishing the *Surrealist Manifesto* in 1924, the surrealist artists emerged, their dream imagery becoming part of popular culture. And in his Manifesto, Breton may have had the vanishing cats, babies morphing into pigs and flamingos used as croquet mallets as described by Dodsgson in mind when he wrote "an unlikely juxtaposition of everyday objects in unexpected places."

GIORGIO DE CHIRICO

Surrealist artist Giorgio de Chirico (1888-1978) painted dream-like townscapes into which he placed strange juxtapositions of inanimate objects, for example, a heap of bananas alongside a marble bust, *The Uncertainty of the Poet* (1913). The violent, sexual and often beautiful images of Salvador Dali (1904-1989) are now ubiquitous; no surprise that he created the dream sequence for Alfred Hitchcock's movie, *Spellbound*, the theme of which was dream analysis. And it is no surprise that the rise and rise of the surrealist poets and artists happened as Sigmund Freud and Carl Jung were writing their books on the subject of dream analysis. Whatever way the surrealist chose to express himself, whether by the extravagant imagery of Dali or the more colloquial, sinister and witty paintings of Renee Magritte, they all had one thing in common.

THE COMMON DENOMINATOR

Through drawing upon the forms of the "real" world, surrealism had dispensed with the portraits and landscapes of "high" art. Now, imagery was used to express the emotion and strangeness of the dream. I could argue here that while you can create a work of art to express a dream, a dream is a creative work of sorts. After all, dreams are fragments of actual experiences, scrambled and reorganised into a weird avatar of reality. This is why I have expressed over and over again, the importance of recording as much dream imagery as is practical. As with beach-combing, you never know what you are going to find or where.

What do we dream about – when, where, about whom?

If the truth be told, we dream, from the words in the poem 'The Walrus and the Carpenter', which is within the text of *Alice Through the Looking Glass* author Lewis Carroll: "of sealing wax and string, of cabbages and kings". And it is not inappropriate that this writer should include in his book a juxtaposition of items such as these because at the end of the book, he reveals that the protagonist, Alice, has actually been dreaming. So, what *else* do we dream about?

Polls on common dreams differ, but only slightly. Overall, the most usual dreams involve being trapped somewhere, falling, being pursued, being lost or losing a precious object. Vehicles, buildings, animals, eating strange substances and finding oneself naked in public are also common dreams. We dream about the places that we know and the places we would love to visit. We dream about fantastical lands that never were and probably never will be.

We dream of the places in which we go to work or go to school, often familiar but with a detail out of place, such as, of all of the sturdy desks in your school classroom or office having been transformed into wobbly marshmallow – or all of your colleagues having had their heads turned around backwards. In dreams, we can feel ecstatically happy or despairingly sad. We dream of people we know well and of people whom we will never meet. We dream of familiar faces either transformed into something new and better, or rendered disfigured and bestial – and yes, we dream of ourselves transformed in various ways. We dream of great riches and extremes of dereliction. We dream of fun and food and famous people, of wide-open prairies and restricting prisons. In dreams, we scale high mountains and dive into deep oceans. We perform tasks which, in reality, we have no skill for. We slay dragons and overturn kingdoms and win glittering prizes. In contrast, we can occupy positions of untenable meniality, like the executive who finds himself polishing floors.

The point is that there is no "average" dream. We all dream about anything and everything. For many years, I experienced constant, recurring dreams that I was hopping into and out of planes, trains and automobiles, usually with the intention of making a journey. But I never seemed to get anywhere, by either missing a travel connection or ending up where I had started from. More about that, later. Whatever we do, wherever we go, whoever we meet, all dreams have one thing in common: while we are dreaming, we *believe* in what is happing.

DREAM CAPTURE

Often, when seeking inspiration to kick-start a piece of work, I trawl through my dream diary and never fail to find material with which to get going once more. Money problems, love problems, work problems – all can be helped or even solved with the information that comes through dreams. And dream information is *free*, sent by your unconscious to your conscious mind, on a plate and without any strings attached. It is the ultimate free gift.

Recording dreams is a task that requires discipline, persistence and dedication, but it is worth the effort. Effective dream analysis is possible only for the routine recorder of dreams, and the most efficient method is to record every dream upon awakening. Keep a jotting pad and pen at your bedside and write down everything you can remember from your dream; encounters with persons known or unknown, the places you visit, details of sounds and colours and if any, your feelings and emotions. Do not forget to record the date the dream took place, as the time of the dream in the context of your life does have a bearing upon its meaning. This recording does take a degree of strategy; if you do not have a room of your own and you wake up in the early hours with a head filled with imagery, then nip out to the bathroom armed with your pen and paper. If you prefer, tell the dream to your telephone – but take care to ensure that no one hears you speaking or can gain access to your records. Later on, I will say much more on the downside of revealing your dream details too soon, to other people. But for now, just take my word for it.

If you really are too muzzy and sleepy to connect your writing fingers with your brain, then just jot down a few key words and phrases that will keep the imagery in your head until you are fully awake, for example, *waterfall, rocks, accident*. Whatever you do, ensure that the chosen phrases will bring your memories flooding back.

THE DREAM NOTEBOOK

In the longer term, a bundle of hastily written notes is not a good device to rely upon. The majority of dreamers like to record their imagery on a more permanent media, such as into a hardcover notebook or onto computer disk. When choosing a notebook, pick a quality item with a tactile cover and spine, and in an attractive (to you) colour. Marbled end-papers and gilt edges are optional, but it is important psychologically to be in possession of a journal that is satisfying to handle and read. When writing, do not forget to add dates. Whether writing or typing onto a keyboard, identify the dream with a title. For example, a burning house filled with tigers against a red sky could be entitled "red hot tigers" or "furry warm day". An encounter with a kitten wearing a necklace could be "puss in jewels" or "pearly kitten". Make use of titles of popular movies and songs, for example, you can title a dream in which it is dark one minute and light the next "Night and Day".

As you practise this craft, the most appropriate words will emerge from your subconscious and in turn, these will solidify into metaphors of the most significant events and people in your life. And the ease with which you become adept at the skill will surprise you. Whichever device you choose, make sure that you have access to a permanent record of written-up dreams. The advantage of a notebook is that you can keep it on a shelf and look into your record of fascinating experiences and memories at any time, and you will find it surprisingly relaxing to read just before you go to sleep. The advantage of typing dream notes onto electronic media is that you can make use of the word search facility to identify recurring themes and archetypes, and enable you to add insights months or even years beyond the event of the original dream – maybe you can use both devices in combo?

Again, this activity does take discipline but the satisfaction on seeing your collection of dream memories grow into a fascinating book or even, collection of books, will make it worthwhile. And once more I stress the importance of recording *every* dream. Extravagant dreams are important, but concentration *only* on these will leave gaps in the total picture of your psyche. If all of your dreams are fabulous and fun-filled then lucky you, but the majority of us receive information through "shorts" likened to news' bulletins, of whispered names and numbers, of half-forgotten fragments of events and feelings. Remember that the object of this exercise is to get in touch with your subconscious, the mechanism responsible for driving the conscious part of you. Your subconscious is just as likely to speak to you through those "little" dreams, as through scenarios of great and momentous events – just think of the lob-sided view of life that would be yours if you only ever watched blockbuster movies?

Keeping a dream diary will give you the ability to chart your dream patterns through the seasons. Many people dream more or rather, *remember* more dream imagery during the summer months, because the shorter and lighter nights trigger off more bouts of the restless state that gives way to dreaming. If this is you, then feel pleased that, just as the bee gathers pollen to make honey, summer is a powerhouse of creative imagery that you can store for future projects. One interesting exercise is to chart the variation between seasons, that is, to see if certain imagery occurs more often in one season. For instance, I notice that my summer dreams are filled with colour – and see my chapter **Cosmic Dreams** for much information about colour in dreams. Of course, a goodly supply of dreams assumes that you are getting enough sleep.

THE BENEFITS OF SLEEPING

The psychological benefits of dreaming parallel those physiological processes that happen to our bodies while we sleep. Hormones essential for the repair of ravaged tissues flood our bloodstreams, and our white blood cell count increases, thus boosting our immune systems.[32] As this repair process progresses, the night wears on and the more NREM-REM cycles that we experience, thus increasing the number of dreams that we are likely to remember. Indeed, routine dreaming can be symptomatic of a person who achieves a deep and healthy sleep.

And if dream interpretation promotes psychological health, then it follows that a sound mind and a healthy body go hand in hand. So, at a physiological level, dreams are indeed *a distillation of memories and experiences, fears and hopes, concatenated into a coded cocktail of experiences that often amuse, frighten and intrigue us,* to stay with my original definition. However, in recent times, we have been bombarded with the notion that it is not good to be idle, that productivity is everything and that sleep is somehow a form of laziness. Indeed, within living memory, a now-deceased prime minister of England made it known that she required only four hours of sleep every night – and stressed her belief that this was somehow a good thing. Even today, many people who feel

---

32   Ian Oswald 'Sleep' in The *Oxford Companion,* p. 718-719.

tired put their condition down to being "fed up" and begin to seek distractions that include mall shopping and spending nights on the town. They take a "holiday" in some exotic resort and party until dawn. They read the latest diet book and embark on some extraordinary nutritional regime. They fill themselves with vitamin pills and listen to sermons on the corroding effect of idleness. They will take up a new hobby, find a new job or even, find a new lover. They will go anywhere and do anything other than admit that they simply need to get more hours of sleep than they actually do get, every night.

THE INSIDIOUS 24/7

In our times, the 24/7 culture has become so entrenched that for a while, it seemed that it might need a complete wiping out and starting over again of humanity to breed a creature who sees sleep as a good thing. Happily, science came to the rescue. In 2017, the Nobel committee awarded its annual prize for medicine to three US scientists who discovered the genes that control our circadian rhythms. Long established in orthodox science, circadian rhythms control our internal modifiers or clocks, the phases that we go through in daily, weekly and even, in yearly cycles.

We all experience times when we feel physical and robust in contrast to times when we prefer to be involved with an intense mental activity like drawing and painting – or just want to be alone with a book. In 2017, these scientists uncovered even more information about this phenomenon.

Formerly, scientists believed that this clock or modifier was just a small bundle of cells that resided in the brain. Moreover, they believed that if you fooled this minute area of the brain into believing that it was daytime, for example, by exposure to ultraviolet light, you could stave off the desire to sleep indefinitely. But their discoveries rendered this theory obsolete. The prize-winning scientists – Jeffrey C. Hall, Michael

Rosbash, and Michael Young – established that Earth's daily revolutions synchronize with a DNA "clock" that resides within every cell in our bodies, a clock that controls our wake and sleep cycles (see **Appendix B**). Paradoxically, you can fool the sophisticated, psychological intellect but not the more primitive organisms that use downtime for repair and renewal. The wonder is that the establishment took that long to make the need for sleep official!

THE TOTAL PICTURE

Come sundown, all areas of your body shut down and prepare for sleep. This makes sense; you cannot fool the tissues in your body into believing that, without having experienced a few hours' sleep, at least, the hormones necessary for growth and repair have been delivered to them. Bruno Bettelheim believed that sleep and in consequence, dream deprivation, was an actual cause of psychological distress: "Recent dream research has shown that a person deprived of dreaming, even though not deprived of sleep, is nevertheless impaired in his ability to manage reality; he becomes emotionally disturbed because of being unable to work out in dreams the unconscious problems that beset him".[33]

It could be that the absence of sleep-time dreaming plays a role in psychological illness. Or it could be that the side-by-side absence of dreaming and psychological illness is co-relational rather than causal, that is, disturbed people do not dream rather than persons suffering from lack of sleep are prone to psychological disturbance. But even if the former case is the truer picture, this still suggests to me that dreaming is a healthy and essential activity. After all, the crippled person knows that it is his afflicted limbs that keep him from walking - and not his inability to walk that has afflicted his limbs. He knows that it is still

---

33   Bettelheim, *The Uses of Enchantment,* p. 63.

good and healthy for him to move about – and so he finds other activity as a substitute for his lack of mobility.

And the Nobel committee's decision, together with the success of Guy Meadows's book *The Sleep Guide: How to Sleep Well Every Night*, has opened a dialogue about the chronic sleep deprivation of the majority of people, about the devastating price we pay for career progress – as opposed to attaining professional excellence – and publicised the many shocking cases like that of the late Miwa Sado, the young Japanese reporter who died of heart failure following undertaking 159 hours of overtime (see **Appendix B**). The key to a healthy mind – and body - is not, it seems, sitting on top of an Asian mountain, drinking yaks' milk as bells ring and monks chant mantras. Nope; you simply (a) switch off light, (b) put head on pillow and (c) close eyes, all as a prelude to eight hours in the land of nod – and not just occasionally, but *every* night. And if only it were as simple as that!

SLEEP-TIME DIFFICULTIES

Many hurdles to sleep abound in our modern world. You may have to work – or play – late into the night. You may have young children keeping you awake, be coping with illness or the constant barking of a neighbour's dog. Or you might be suffering from good, old-fashioned insomnia. Since very few of us control our lives entirely, these circumstances are often difficult to deal with. But bearing in mind that sufficient sleep is essential to physical and psychological health, what you must do initially, is see a good night's sleep as an obtainable goal, and not a mere indulgence. Health, sleep and dreams are all intertwined and the Nobel committee's decision has opened a conversation about the chronic sleep deprivation of many people, and the need to recognise sleep not as an indulgence or extravagance, but as a tool vital for optimum health. If you have problems sleeping or even, finding time to sleep, make use of the following steps to break the habit – *now.*

SEE SLEEP AS AN ENTITLEMENT, NOT AS AN INDULGENCE OR LUXURY

Do *not* be taken in by the school that teaches that bed is only for the desperately ill or the terminally exhausted. Recognise now that you are entitled to a night's sleep. Quality shut-eye is vital for optimum mental and physical activity, and should not be the reserve of an elite. If you have to work overtime for a period, then negotiate for extra days off of work when the rush is over. Pool childminding duties with partners, relatives and friends; trading time is not begging a favour. Tell your partying friends that you are taking time out to catch up on sleep.

DO CHECK OUT THE PERSONAL CONUNDRUMS THAT KEEP YOU AWAKE AT NIGHT

It could be that you are frustrated in your role at work. Changing jobs or taking a course to improve your career prospects will enhance your life in every direction. You may be in a relationship that you want to say bye-bye to. Or an unwelcome suitor is foisting their attentions upon you. Bearing in mind the difference between constant disturbance and one-off events, take action against noisy neighbours. It is all easier said than done, of course, but practical intervention and total honesty, no matter how unpleasant, is the likeliest solution to tackling situations like these. And you *will* sleep better at night.

CHECK YOUR ENVIRONMENT

Review your sleeping environment and remove all distractions to shut-eye. This could mean moving a television set or other electronic items from the bedroom. Get rid of photographs of relatives – pleasant though they are to look at – and other images whose presence you cannot ignore. With the clutter vanquished, redecorate the room in gentle colours, pale blues and pinks, lilac, cream and green. Buy the finest bedding that you can afford; pile the bed with pillows – lavender-scented are the most restful. Take steps to ensure that your room is never too warm or too cold.

DO GET PLENTY OF EXERCISE DURING THE DAY

Train your body to *want* to sleep. Walking, cycling and swimming – add your favourite activity here – are all healthy pastimes that pull oxygen into the lungs and thus to all areas of the body, via the bloodstream. Exercise builds muscle and helps keep it toned. It keeps weight in check and helps induce that sleepy yet relaxed feeling that betokens plenty of shut-eye, just before bedtime. But do not exercise *too* close to bedtime, which can have the opposite effect.

DO NOT EAT OR DRINK HEAVILY AFTER **8** PM

Avoid heavy meals too close to bedtime. Once you eat, you set your digestive system in motion, a process that definitely interferes with sound sleep. Take your main daily meal at lunchtime, if possible. If this is not possible, try to finish supper by 8 pm. If you must eat afterwards, try a light snack of wholemeal toast and a piece of fruit; do not add a heavy protein filling, like meat, fish or cheese. Whatever you do, do *not* get in the habit of taking alcohol just before bedtime. The resulting alcohol-induced fug is not the same as natural, healthy sleep.

DO LOOK AT THE HERB FAMILY

Certain herbal infusions are renowned for helping the body relax, which can only lead to enhanced sleep. Look in a health food store for teas of chamomile and marshmallow, coriander and vervain, sweet violet and bergamot. You will probably find that combinations of these leaves work best. Experiment until you find the one that is most effective for you. The scent of lavender is renowned for inducing sleep; place a pillow filled with lavender petals on your bed and top up the scent occasionally with a dab of lavender oil.

TAKE A CALMING BATH AND LISTEN TO RELAXING MUSIC

Develop a bedtime routine. Even if you don't feel sleepy, begin preparing for bed around the same time every night. Post 8pm, soften the lights and turn down the music – do *not* reach for that glass of alcohol. At about 10pm, take a warm shower and pull on that glam nightie or those swanky jammies. If you must read, choose a few pages of a relaxing book before shutting your eyes. Again, ritual helps. Many an insomniac has found that simply turning out the light and lying still in darkness can induce a deep and healthy sleep.

WITH RESERVATIONS, TAKE A VACATION

No pun intended. Be careful of leaving workaday cares behind; the purpose of this information is to help you sleep in your *usual* environment. But there is a case for taking an occasional vacation and discovering how the rarefied conditions of a comfortable hotel room and exotic climate can work together to promote sleep. Beforehand, decide *why* you want to get away; a very stimulating environment will inhibit sleep, as will the party-all-night type of vacation.

GO TO A SLEEP CLINIC

This measure may seem extreme, but if you are suffering from the type of insomnia that the above raft of measures will not cure, then it is advisable to seek medical help. If constant nightmares interrupt your sleep or if you suspect you are sleepwalking, then ask your medical practitioner for referral to a sleep clinic. Luckily, common sleep disorders respond well to treatment.

DREAM FAQS

Here, I attempt to answer a number of the most common questions that people ask about dreams and dreaming. It is not possible to raise all questions, let alone answer them thoroughly. But the following headlines will enable the attentive student of this book to answer his or her own questions.

HOW OFTEN SHOULD WE DREAM?

How long is a piece of string? Given that we experience between six and eight NREM-REM sleep cycles every night, we probably experience between six and eight dreams every time we go to sleep. However, *remembering* dreams is another matter. The majority of us, when we remember a dream at all, can only recall those dreams we have experienced immediately before we wake up, usually in the final one or two NREM-REM cycles. This means that we forget most of the dreams that we experience. However, since the longer periods of REM – and those more dramatic dreams – do happen towards morning, we can learn much from the dreams that we *do* remember.

CAN I INFLUENCE MY DREAMS?

This is a difficult one to tackle; the short answer is "yes" but be aware, like the mythical three wishes, the results that you achieve might not be what you had in mind. Racy dreams are often the result of lying in a foetal position, while many pleasant dreams stem from a fortunate real-time experience, the preceding day. You can play music as you fall asleep, put flowers on your bedside table or watch a favourite television show or movie while in bed, in the hope that the action with George Clooney, Nicole Kidman or whoever, will continue into the sleeping hours. These exercises are fun, certainly, and may well stave off nightmares, but...

Bear in mind that the main purpose of dream analysis is to gain access to your subconscious mind for the material that will help you to take control of your life. Trying to manipulate your dream material might obfuscate this purpose. That said, there is a case for limited dream manipulation, which I outline in my section, *Lucid Dreaming*.

After all, I can listen to favourite music or watch a movie any time; sleep time is for channelling those precious snippets of information that could make all the difference between success or failure, misery or happiness, in a particular area of life. If you are in dire need of a storyline for a creative writing class, try putting a stuffed monkey, an empty beer bottle and a crystal necklace on your dresser – the results could be surprising.

But be aware that too much "stuff" in the sleeping environment, including cluttered dressing tables, the buzz of telephones and televisions alike will only block off those vital signals from the subconscious required when solving a personal conundrum. Here, I concur with dream whisperer Davina MacKail in refusing to entertain electronic equipment in my bedroom.[34] And yes, Mary Shelley did get the plot of *Frankenstein* in a dream, but be aware that that author lead an eventful and liberal lifestyle, and that she had attended a lecture on galvanic electricity only months before she created her famous bit-part man. And never forget that all of the information you need to live a successful life is already there, dormant in your subconscious and active when you sleep, just waiting for you to harvest it. And this topic begs the next question: can I *stop* dreams from coming in?

CATCHING DREAMS

Until now, I have outlined the necessity of *dream capture* as opposed to *catching* dreams – and stopping them from manifesting. The dreamcatcher originated among the Ojibwe, a Native American tribe. According to their folklore, the Asibikashi or Spider Woman protected the people of the tribe on their own lands. When they began to disseminate to all areas of the North American landmass, Spider Woman lost this power. The women of the tribe began to weave web-like items out of willow hoops and cord for hanging over the cots and beds of their children, to

---

34 McKail, *The Dream Whisperer*, p. 24.

"catch" bad dreams and only let the nice dreams through. (see **Appendix B**) As with many other cultural tropes, the dreamcatcher moved beyond its origins and into the capitalist mainstream, eventually reaching the pages of a Stephen King novel.

In photographs, dreamcatchers are delicate, pretty and feather-ornamented items, belying their rather dark purpose. Given what I know about it, I believe that the effectiveness of a dreamcatcher works by the age-old power of suggestion. Tell the subject that the dreamcatcher will prevent his nightmares (see **Dream Disorders**) and he will fall asleep in a less anxious frame of mind, less stressed or even less frightened, which are the states of mind that often underlie bad dreams, and he is less likely to have – a bad dream. But this is not the only reason I have never dashed to the nearest novelty shop to purchase a Native American object. I believe that all dream information is significant and symptomatic, even that received in "bad" dreams. Pinpoint the archetypes of the imagery, and you are on the way to finding both cause and cure.

Of course, I am self-aware enough to deal with any disturbing material that filters through. As I point out in the chapter, **Dream Disorders**, anyone who is suffering seriously with a sleep disorder should seek professional help. But I *do* have a dreamcatcher; it's called a *pen* - with a nice writing pad attached!

LUCID DREAMS

Lucid dreaming is a subject that I do not often wax lyrical upon, because I am hopelessly inept at driving my own nighttime imagery. Basically, a lucid dream is one in which the dreamer knows that he or she is dreaming and is able to take control of the events. Davina MacKail describes a technique with which to grow competent at it, namely, choosing a familiar

35 McKail, *The Dream Whisperer*, p. 179.

object that is about you daily and concentrating upon it, at intervals.[35] When the object inevitably appears in your dreams it is bound to be a little altered, and you will know that you are dreaming, ergo you can remind yourself of this fact, and use the awareness to gain control of events. I have tried this technique, but in vain, However, I do have an effective mechanism for controlling dream imagery. Read on.

TAKE HEART, WALTER MITTY...

When I was young, I was forever getting called up for my habit of *daydreaming* at school and later on, at work. What I could never (still don't) understand was how a body – or mind – could get through an average day without a few bouts of least, of that most creative of mental states. And I still don't understand why daydreaming carries such a negative tag, especially when I get my best ideas when not actively pursuing any "conscious" task. And I am not alone; a daydream while on a train journey prompted JK Rowling to embark on her uber-celebrated *Harry Potter* series of books.

Psychologists have written much on the nature of daydreaming. The majority of them seem to agree that while daydreaming, the subject is in a state between waking and sleeping. And while asleep, the subject is in touch with his or her subconscious. Detached from the automotive mode of consciousness, the daydream is the ideal place for thoughts to flow. Even when a daydream does not result in a great and wonderful idea – most often, it does not – experts agree (and daydreaming subjects affirm) that a short period of detachment from the conscious state is akin to taking a quick nap.

More often than not, the subject returns to consciousness, fully capable of tackling whatever task is in hand. One difference between the dreams of day and those of the night is that the daydreaming subject has slightly more control over the imagery that he or she receives, which provides potential for great creativity. Again and again, descent into the imagination has enabled man to create the world's more remarkable and curious inventions and works of art.

Dream Archetypes

One point that I had ever noticed about dreams were those recurring motifs and people that occupied nighttime dramas, albeit in different situations. Determined to make sense of it all, I began to read. And read. And read. My material included *The Dream Whisperer* by Davina MacKail and *The Uses of Enchantment: The Meaning and Importance of Fairy Tales* by Bruno Bettelheim.[36]

And what I uncovered was game-changing; I will forever be indebted to these writers for my knowledge of dream archetypes. Even today, identifying dream archetypes is an activity that always sends shivers up and down my spine. It is like that moment in a movie when the hero or heroine opens a mysterious door or closet to reveal...whatever. It is the equivalent of opening the Pandora's box to your own psyche. What you discover will not always be reassuring, but it will be authentic and empowering – and power is what we are after here – and what exactly, is an archetype?

In a nutshell, dream archetypes are those images and characters that appear over and over again, in various dream situations, over a period of time – just think of the same character type appearing in many different plays and movies – the goodie and baddie, the hero and lovers? For years, I would wake up, convinced that I had dreamed at least once before of the character or the event that I had just been dreaming about. Until I began to keep a dream diary, I had no way of finding out. When I eventually began my diary, I began to classify these

---

36   McKail, *The Dream Whisperer*, p. 108.

events and characters, which became my stock of archetypes. And that begs the question of why stock images and characters are so significant?

In my chapter, **The Fairy Tale, Literature & Art** I mentioned stock characters, you know, the princes and princesses, wicked stepmothers, giants and witches, that seem common to all fairy tales and of how these characters embody the hopes and fears of the very young. The *prince* and the *princess* are the ideal versions of ourselves, the person or personas that we want to be, following the journey that we all make through growth and maturity. Wicked stepmothers, giants, witches and other "monster" characters embody all of the obstacles and other unsavoury events that we are bound to endure while on our individual quests. Over time, the study of dreams in conjunction with the deeper meanings of the fairy tale has convinced me that our body of popular folklore has grown from the nighttime phantasms of countless generations of dreamers. The more popular fairy tales have travelled intact through time because the archetypes they contain are universal, common to all cultures. The stories contain characters and elements that we all respond to…just think of the plot of any favourite movie?

Another of my convictions is that all of the folklore of the world has grown from the dreams of the people who spin the tales; just consider Greek mythology, filled with sunny, daytime people and shadowy, nocturnal figures, winged horses, chariots that cross the sky by day, messengers with winged heels, magic cloaks and helmets, and so much more. Essentially, myths are individual dreams that have solidified into collective imagination, which is why I have provided a selection of these at the end of this section. If you prefer, you can liken dream archetypes to the symbols that are found on Tarot cards. In this very old from of fortune telling, the symbols were derived from the archetypes that existed in the lives of the people that created them. Every town had its rich man and poor man – or men, its beauty, and its busybody and its idiot. In our modern times, archetypes are everywhere, though maybe not identifiable in our less close-knit society. In our dreams, archetypes are the images that pop up again and again – and perish the thought that these are just random and useless pieces of information floating to the surface of consciousness.

HOW TO MAKE USE OF THE ARCHETYPE

We are all possessed of an "inner self", a core of being, a self that never changes, made up of qualities, standards and morals, that our individual experiences and environments have endowed us with. However, this untouchable self is not enough on its own to enable us to master the "real" world. As adults, we regard ourselves as "grown up" but in reality, we continually mature throughout life. Life around us changes whether we want it to or not. We encounter new people, new difficulties and indeed, new opportunities, and we need to learn how to respond to these changes. In order to gain control over our lives, we need to respond effectively to the outer world, developing the less obvious aspects of our personalities, brushing up on old skills and even, discovering hidden talents. Dream archetypes behave as the hidden aspects of our own personalities, aspects that are trying to communicate something significant to us. It is by identifying these archetypes, decoding the information that they are conveying to us and acting upon it, that we achieve personal growth.

HOW TO BEGIN

This is why you should begin identifying dream archetypes as soon as you can. I did not begin the process until I had been capturing dreams for a number of years, a mistake on my part. But then, I was unaware of the power of archetype identification, and the treasure trove of insights that it was to place at my fingertips.

The first part of the process is, essentially, the same as dream capture. Keep a notebook and pen at your bedside and record every dream upon awakening. Note down all of the people in it, explaining who they are if you know them, and a description of the person if unknown. Describe all events, colours and sounds, and how you felt while everything was "happening". Most importantly, record any words you heard spoken or saw written in the dream. I had only been doing this exercise for a few weeks when I noticed patterns emerging, certain stock characters that appeared in my various nocturnal dramas, like familiar actors in different plays. But really, how soon should you begin to identify your archetypes?

If (like me) you capture a good dream twice or three times every week, and you have been keeping a diary for at least one month, then you will have between nine and twelve good dreams to play with. As your dream diary builds, you will begin to see patterns emerging. You really will find that there is nothing "accidental" about the images that haunt your sleep. If you keep your diary on a computer, you will find the word search a marvellous facility. Read through this material occasionally and you will almost certainly find one recurring trope. It could be a "dark man", a "fair woman" or an "old house"?

My dreams often involve a blonde female subject and because I am fair, I can identify with this person. In a recurring dream a few years ago, the blonde woman kept appearing before me with beautiful and abundant hair; unfortunately, I am not possessed of her luxuriant tresses. After much analysis, I worked out that the blonde woman was telling me that *my assets were greater than I imagined*. She was right.

ANALYSING ARCHETYPES

Identifying archetypes is one matter, of course, but analysing them and deciding what they are trying to communicate to you, is another matter. Happily, there is a technique for that. If you are new to keeping a dream diary, do collect a few dream tropes before you begin the following exercise. One question that readers often ask is: how do you know if an archetype really is an archetype, and that it is not just an image accidentally appearing in a number of dreams?

One good way of telling is by questioning the nature of your feelings surrounding the recurring dream emblem? Remember that dream interpretation is intuitive. If you continually dream about, say, a dark man and a number of animals, and you are absolutely bursting with curiosity over the dark man in your waking hours, then you can be certain that this *is* the archetype, that he has information to communicate to you. For the present, disregard the animals – unless you have a strong feeling concerning one or more of them. You can use the following method, a method that I developed over a period of time. Before you begin, be aware that simply sitting and thinking about an image is a limited and intimidating way to spin; at least, I find it so. This is possibly because the conscious mind is trying to "hide" the meaning of a particular dream or archetype from you, most likely the reason why your subconscious is sending you disguised imagery, to begin with. The best way to spin an image is to bring your conscious and subconscious minds in tandem with one another, but while staying awake. And relaxation is the best way to do this.

Assume a relaxed posture either sitting or lying down and as with dream capture, have writing materials waiting alongside you. People who meditate routinely will find the process easier to do, post meditation. In fact, the time immediately after meditating is ideal for analysing a dream image. Think about the image that recurs in your dream. If, for example, it is an oyster, think about the connotations surrounding the word: hard shell, shellfish, tasty, desirable, luxury, worldly, world is your oyster – and so on. Remember, there are no "right" or "wrong" answers.

Decide what the word means *to you*. When you have so many ideas that you feel you can't hold back from writing them down, do so. Of course, the longer you work with a dream image, the better chance you have of deciphering its underlying meaning. For a businessman, the oyster may be the archetype of the success he desires. He might dream that he is trying to flip open each oyster with a knife and failing in each attempt. He then finds another, stronger knife and he succeeds in opening the oyster. His dream is telling him to try another, stronger tactic to make more sales. Of course, the knife is another dream archetype and the more of these you gather and learn to interpret, the better your dream analysis will be. If your archetype is a character, then in the relaxation exercise, picture the dream character and ask him or her questions: who are you, what do you do, what are you trying to tell me?

Note any and every word that comes into your head as you study the person. For example, if your archetype is a dark man, your words may be "stranger", "handsome", "prince", "mystery", "love", "romance" and so on. Of course, the meanings that come to you will vary according to your gender, age and condition in life. Later, write down every word you think of and – I always find this so exciting - at some point, you will suddenly realise what the character is trying to communicate. It is important to remember that the dream archetype is an aspect of your own personality, not another, intrusive individual. For example, the young woman who keeps dreaming of a dark and handsome man may find that her dream subject is the part of her that is longing for adventure. It does not (sadly) mean that a dark and handsome man is about to enter her life. And a man may find that the male stranger who appears in his dream is the competitive, go-getting part of himself.

It is in the information received during the lighter hours of sleep that we can identify our attitudes to everything; attitudes that may be holding us back from success in work, making money, love – everything. And I warn readers once more against speaking freely of the imagery that you receive. This information is far too precious to relay to everyone we meet, which is why the subconscious sends it to us in the imagery that we call dreams. Indeed, such relaying of the psyche could leave us vulnerable if the information gets into the wrong hands, so treat dream imagery for what it is, highly personal information from your subconscious and meant only for you.

REPLENISHING YOUR STOCK

Routinely adding to your stock of archetypes with imagery that recurs in your dreams is important and is the long-term route to expertise in dream analysis. The more you "spin" your archetype, that is, the more connections you can generate with an image, the more in-depth will be your insight into your dream. It is a skill that takes time to master. Persisting with this capture can only bring forward the day when you are in possession of a library of archetypes, a key into the fascinating world of your own subconscious. When you become really adept at this technique, then you can encourage your stock characters to "talk" to one another, a technique that I describe in a later chapter.

DREAM CYCLES OR DREAM ARCHETYPES?

One matter that often confuses dreamers is the difference between dream archetypes and dream cycles. Many people are prone to dreaming during the crossroads of life; the career changes and marriages, the births and the deaths. Many women find that their menstrual cycle affects their dreaming, something you can ascertain by dating your dreams. Here, we are concerned with the archetypes that appear during the mundane stages of life. Remember that our dream archetypes are unique to ourselves; the dream of a racing car will mean something quite different to a driver than to a person who has never sat in a driving seat. All the same, in the following section, I provide a selection of the more mundane archetypes that have assisted me throughout my creative life.

THE FAIR WOMAN

One figure that keeps appearing in my dreams, especially when I am going through lean times, is the fair-haired or blonde woman. Although

I envy her beauty, I always welcome her appearance as she is a sign that things are going to improve. In Greek mythology, the fair woman parallels with the "daytime" goddesses, strong women who like hunting, gathering and other productive activities. One of these fair women is the corn goddess, Demeter, associated with the invention of the mill and the raising of vegetables. She is often portrayed seated with torches and a serpent. Another fair woman is Athena, who presides over art and literature, over spinning, weaving and household activities. She is also a warrior goddess, wearing a helmet and carrying a shield. Artemis, twin sister of the sun god, Apollo, is another hunter. Whoever the fair woman is, she stands for energy, abundance and action.

THE DARK WOMAN

A young, dark woman often appears in my dreams, usually as a cautionary official. Once, she served me food in a restaurant. Hecate is the dark twin of Artemis, credited with the invention of sorcery. She has the power to grant material prosperity, eloquent speech and victory in competition. Hecate is the mother of another dark lady, Circe. She is the enchantress who lured the Greek warriors returning from Troy, led by Odysseus, into her palace. As they ate and drank her food and wine, she waved her magic wand and they changed into swine. The appearance of the dark woman in a dream is a warning to beware of forthcoming gifts or good fortune that comes too easily.

THE OLD MAN

In several of my dreams, an old man has appeared, an indicator that my life is moving from one phase to another. In one dream, I found an old man lying asleep or dead, in my bed. In dreams, death is the symbol of imminent change. In Greek mythology, old Autolycus is the grandfather of Odysseus, and has the power to shape-shift, with the ability to change himself into an animal. He is also a notorious thief. Another old man is

Silvanus, a Roman deity of the woods. He possesses the strength of youth and his mysterious voice is known always to tell the truth.

THE CHILD

It is always touching to meet a child that you know, in a dream. However, several of my dreams have featured unknown children, the archetype of areas of my life that I have never explored. Some years ago when I was recovering from illness, I had a dream about a group of children who were heading towards a swimming pool. I remember thinking: I must dive into a new career when I recover. I did, and exploring the depths has served me well. The most famous child in mythology is Eros or Cupid, the personification of love. Many legends surround the birth of Eros. In his *Symposium*, Plato describes Eros as having been born from the union of Expediency (Poros) and Poverty (Penia). He is not powerful but is a perpetually restless and dissatisfied force.

THE REVELLER

A number of my dreams have featured a particular relative who was very fond of merry-making and partying. Indeed, when he appears in my dreams, we are most often at a party or some kind of celebration. His appearance is the archetype of *old emotions that hamper new progress*. This could be progress either in work or in relationships. The most renowned reveller in Greek mythology is Bacchus or Dionysus, god of the vine and Lord of Misrule, the son of Zeus and Semele. He wandered around the countryside accompanied by his triumphal train, the Bacchantes, the Sileni, the Satyrs and other minor deities. Wherever he brought his revels, entire populations – especially of women – were seized by madness. Dreams featuring the Reveller are a warning against being dragged down by old or negative emotions.

THE CROWD

Occasionally, I have a dream that is populated by a crowd of shadowy people; indistinguishable as individuals, like the chorus familiar to Greek comedy and tragedy. A crowd in my dreams in the archetype of *conforming*, a group of people who assemble to mourn or rejoice. Whatever, they always do the same thing. It is the context of the dream that determines whether I should conform or strike my own path. Some time ago, I was confronted with a decision of whether or not to pursue a particular training course. Then, I dreamed that I was seated on a beach with a crowd of people, all of us munching on chocolate eggs. The dream was warning me to avail of the opportunity or else be deprived of benefits that everyone else was enjoying. In the longer term, I did the course and it has served me well ever since. And this is only a small selection of possible archetypes.

Meditative Exercises

THE DREAM GUIDE

The career of Australian writer Robert Moss began when he dreamed of an Iroquois woman and from her, learned advanced dreaming techniques – hmmm. If you have had a similar experience, then lucky you. Alas, no dream shaman has ever favoured me; I've learned everything the laborious way, collecting dreams, pin-pointing archetypes and interpreting them according to the information revealed.

And for a very long time, I was determined to avoid the hoary old "spirit of a Native Indian" cliché. I was determined to do the work and no-one else need lend a hand. After all, who knows you better than *you* do? The answer, they say, lies in the question and, in spite of my determination to keep it in the family, my dream guides came to me, one by one, over time. Experiencing the emergence of dream guides is a little like an introduction to relatives whom you have never met, and with whom you develop a rich and ultimately rewarding relationship. The essence of dreaming is that the less developed parts of the personality spring into conversation with the more familiar areas of the self. When you identify and engage with these unknown areas, then you have the mechanism to develop a more rounded personality.

THE NEW RELATIVES

My connecting with my guides began when I noticed that many of my dreams featured a dark female who often seemed in conflict with whatever purpose I was following – in the dream. Gradually, I realised that her presence was there to challenge my point of view in whatever situation I was in – in waking hours. Also, she was my opposite in every sense because I am fair. So, I created the dark Phonecia, thus my "dark woman" whom I described in the earlier section.

I christened an older, avuncular male "the old man" Magnus, his name, of course, being a play on the word "magus", which occurred to me after listening to a radio broadcast of Shakespeare's play, *The Tempest*. Throughout the broadcast, I envied Miranda having the wise Prospero to instruct and guide her. Later on, I created the silver-bright Fortuna. Named after a Roman goddess who is associated with material prosperity, she wears a tall headdress that looks like an illuminated city. Incidentally, many British towns have had a shrine to Fortuna since Roman times, including the one I live in. Mercury is a come-lately to my committee table. Like a city gent, he wears a bowler hat and suit, and I call upon him to help me with the smooth running of financial and legal affairs. Over time, Magnus, Phonecia and the others have become like friends, oracles to consult when I am uncertain of a course to take in a personal or professional matter. Primarily, they are guides through the world of imagination, and help me bring what I discover there to the waking world. But how does it all work?

PATHWAY TO DREAMS

Use the following exercise when you want to take a step further into dream analysis. You may want to question how a dream symbol or archetype fits into the context of a particular dream – or you may want to try to continue the events of a dream that ended abruptly, and to draw closer to its meaning. To derive maximum benefit from the exercise, place yourself in the same relaxed state of mind that I advocate when spinning out dream archetypes.

Picture yourself walking through a wood, a dark wood. Feel the fallen leaves underfoot and see the branches overhead, with patches of blue sky in between. Hear the sounds; the whisperings of the leaves as you walk, the scampering of small animals dashing into the undergrowth, the occasional burst of birdsong.

As you walk, the dim, dense forest becomes lighter and brighter. The trees grow fewer in number and more and more sky is revealed. Eventually, you arrive at the edge of the forest, the sound of rushing water fills your ears and you see a wide, fast-flowing stream in front of you. Looking about quickly, you see a bridge and on the other side of the stream, a brightly-lit town centre. Six, stone steps lead up to the bridge and count them as you climb: one – two – three – four – five – six.

Here, I chose six because of the association of the number with the "sixth" sense and higher perception, but you can choose a number that is meaningful to you. Cross the bridge, feeling the stonework underfoot as you do so, and descend the steps on the other side, counting again as you do so.

Look out for traffic as you cross the road in front of you and step onto the path. By now, you are in front of the first store window. Through the wide pane of glass you can see a range of delicious foods (see your favourites here) and feel your mouth water as you look at them. Move on to the next window and look through the glass and see the most beautiful clothes, garments that you long to wear. Imagine yourself touching soft wools and velvets and feel soft cottons and satin against your skin. And just imagine your feet in those fine leather shoes and luxurious sandals. The next store is filled with the jewellery that you want to wear, extravagant watches, elegant pearls and sparkling diamonds, the finest of craftsmanship in gold and silver. And your nose tingles to the exotic scents that emanate from the perfumiers, sandalwood and jasmine and vetiver, with wonderful concoctions for the bath sitting in crystal bottles in the window. If you are an artist, picture a gallery filled with paintings by you, while writers can imagine a bookshop, the shelves lined with books bearing your name and titles, along the spines.

Eventually, you arrive at your venue; here, you can choose the place you like to meet and talk to friends. It could be a public house, a private club or a favourite restaurant, but mine is one of those wonderful, art deco coffee shops, redolent of the 1950s, with gleaming chrome spigots and white cups and plates along dark counters. Here, my dream counsellors are waiting for me and I sit down, and we begin to talk.

I don't need to speak to every one of my counsellors, every time. Usually, I present the question that is pressing most to the appropriate counsellor. When I need someone to challenge my opinion, usually when a perceived solution to a situation seems too simple, I ask Phonecia. When I consider it important to call upon the "male" aspects of my own personality, I call upon Magnus. When I begin to fall short on creativity, I apply to Fortuna's counsel. When I get in a tangle with a financial or legal matter, Mercury is at hand. Occasionally, one of the counsellors presents me with a nugget of wisdom that I have not even asked for. When the meeting is over, I thank my counsellors, bid farewell, cross the bridge again and work my way back through the wood. As soon as I emerge from the meditative state, I write down my material so that I do not forget it.

But you don't have to go into "my" town centre; you can follow a rope bridge to a jungle filled with exciting plants and animals, kayak down a waterway to a lost city filled with ruined temples and oracles, climb up a mountain to look down on the four corners of the earth– the ideas are legion and you can derive great enjoyment from creating your own personal world. And because the exercise is imaginary, you need place no limits upon the number and type of counsellors that emerge. The four I describe above are my "core" team, but there are others that emerge and vanish for a while, according to my changing needs. Be aware all the time that any dream counsellors that emerge are personifications of aspects of your own subconscious.

It is through the dramas enacted by these facets or aspects of our personalities that we can more effectively interpret dream meanings. And the more you communicate with them, the better you will know your own capabilities. So, sift systematically through your dream diary. Pinpoint those archetypes and begin assembling your own, personal committee today. I guarantee you a fascinating trip.

MY OWN EXPERIENCE

Many times, I have experienced the frustrating phenomenon of awakening from a dream, just as (I felt) something of significance was about to happen – or I was on the brink of receiving important information. A number of years ago, I had a dream that I eventually named "Behind the Wallpaper." In it, I was in a ticket office, somewhere in the US, trying to buy a ticket to some place. The ticket system kept failing and I ended up holding a blank sheet of paper after which, annoyingly, I woke up. But the phrase "behind the wallpaper" remained in my head and I just knew that this phrase was the key to the unresolved dream.

In my dream-analysis trance, I returned my mental state to the point where I received the sheet of blank paper. I told the ticket system that I was not impressed with its condition, i.e., withholding information, and to please resolve the task. Next, I explored all that wallpaper stood for: design, domestic comfort, and so on. Later that week, I received a variety of leads to possible freelance writing assignments, one of which was from an interior design firm. Although there were other more likely-sounding leads in the list, I remembered my dream, applied for the job – and got it – and yes, the client was based in the US. And this was not the first time that dream information has helped me jump the queue for interesting and well-paid work.

THE GESTALT TECHNIQUE

In my chapter, **Philosophy of Dreams**, I briefly described the subject of Gestalt, that process by which our brains make a "whole" out of an incomplete picture. At a conscious level, we do this quite successfully in our environments. But making sense of the fragmentary images that dreams give us, is quite another skill. To quote psychologist Kurt Koffka, once more: "the whole is other than the sum of its parts."

As I have stressed again and again, until you train your conscious faculty to successfully interpret imagery from the subconscious, you are likely to misunderstand the information that it is trying to relay to you or, more likely, not interpret it at all. Gestalt is a fascinating and absorbing way of gaining skill with this process. Essentially, it consists of questioning all of the symbols that appear in your dream, personifying even inanimate objects and questioning what role or roles that they assume in your waking life.

For example, you have a dream about a suitcase. Begin the analysis by asking the image what it is and what it does, in reality? You open and shut a suitcase. You put things into it and take them out again. You take a suitcase on journeys, putting it upon luggage racks and on and off conveyor belts. The suitcase seems to lead an exciting life, filled with travel and information – but the suitcase has no will of its own; it is passive, used and pushed about by other people. A dream about a suitcase could be an indication that you have taken a passive role in a situation in which you imagined that you were in control or indeed, in which you could possibly take control of. A good Gestalt practitioner will bring you through exercises in which you "talk" to the suitcase, working out how to improve your situation. But if you do not have access to a practitioner, you can put analysis of a dream object or situation into practice with one of your dream counsellors.

INDIVIDUATION: BRINGING THE UNCONSCIOUS
INTO THE CONSCIOUS

In my **Introduction**, I described how Carl Jung added a process called *individuation* to psychoanalysis, that is, healing the person by identifying and developing underdeveloped personality traits, thus achieving a better balance. Individuation is concerned with *bringing the unconscious into the conscious* for the better functioning of the self. Jung theorized that the self was a tripartite construction of *ego*, *conscious* and *unconscious*. He taught that the ego is merely the facet of the self that we reveal to others, and that its healthy functioning depends upon communication between the conscious and the unconscious. The better the communication, the healthier is the person and personality. Curiously, I went through my first individuation experience while I was still a child, before I had ever heard of Jung or Freud, psychoanalysis or the unconscious. A classmate at the school that I went to refused continually to let me take part in playground games with other children. When I tried to do so, she screamed and screamed until, well, until I was thoroughly frustrated and exasperated. I tried but failed to find out why she behaved in this way, and my complaints to Teacher went unheard. It was a horrible time that spilled over into my sleeping hours. Yet, night after night, I dreamed that I ignored the dictates of this kid and joined the playgroups. One, fine spring day, I did just that, ignoring her taunts and screams as I joined a playground chain. That child had no power over me after that and ever after, I took my rightful place in the games of the other children. In summary, the dream to assert my will was the *unconscious* part of me speaking to my *conscious* mind, which, in turn, prompted my *ego* to assert itself.

Years down the line, I still refuse to accept unreasonable behaviour by remaining steadfast, silent and doing what I believe is right. Now, however, I make conscious use of individuation. Whenever I am going through a trauma, where I am trying to achieve something or get my opinion across and am fraught with difficulty, I put me in the meditative state and pose a series of questions to my subconscious – or counsellors - and await the answer(s) in the form of dream imagery.

Just recently, I faced a crossroads about a professional issue that obliged me to wonder whether I should continue the work that I am doing now or return to a former line of work and the way of life that accompanied it. Following a dream counsellor consultation, I dreamed that I was in the centre of a town that I knew well, but that I had left, a long time ago. I wandered into an arena of wooden paling that surrounded a mucky field and bumped into a former boss. Together, we tried to find a way out. Although the meaning of this dream is crystal-clear – do not attempt to return to the past – gaining competence at individuation is not easy.

A number of years ago, I experienced a series of dreams about *snow* and it was through individuation I discovered that my subconscious was advising me to rediscover *hidden talents* – a situation that had a happy resolution. The majority of us know that we could be more successful in work and relationships if we could only be a little more assertive, energetic or find the time to learn a new skill; how hard then is it to develop a trait that you don't even *know* that you have – but it is far from impossible. The unconscious mind has the ability to synthesize and symbolize a "map" of the conscious world. When you interpret this map successfully and put into use the information it sends – whether in a playground, office or family situation – then you are using Jung's process of individuation. And even today, I still feel a modicum of gratitude towards that selfish and silly child for helping me uncover personal strengths that I had been unaware of.

The Children of an Idle Brain

Now, I have arrived at the most exciting part of this book, the part where you begin to "listen in" to all of those dreams, to begin to analyse all of those fascinating sequences and symbols that you have been filling your diaries with. You are now ready to begin making use of them to improve your life – and not a few of you will be well placed to improve the lives of others. Obviously, the more dreams you have collected, the more comprehensive an understanding that you will gain of your inner life. But it is never too soon to begin dream analysis because, once you *have* begun, you will not want to stop. First, there are a number of matters to be aware of.

UNIVERSAL AND PERSONAL SYMBOLS

No matter how much we analyse a dream image and succeed in pinning it to a personal archetype, certain dream symbols will always be universal in meaning. Be aware also that dream interpretation is about context, that arriving at its meaning involves interpreting the other images that you see. Like Carl Jung, I believe that much of the meaning surrounding a dream symbol depends upon the culture in which the dreamer is born into, the age of the subject, the state of health and other social circumstances.

Wild animals symbolise vitality, strength and power, a matter that advertisers are aware of and older readers will remember the slogan for petrol buyers "put a tiger in your tank". Finding yourself allied with a wild beast in a dream is a sign that you have great expectations and a belief that you can achieve them, a prerequisite to much personal gain.

Gold will always be a universal symbol of beauty and long-lasting value. Be aware, however, that the meaning of a dream of wealth shifts according to the status of the dreamer. If a wealthy person dreams of spending money copiously on objects of desire, such as fancy cars and designer clothes, then he is just dreaming of what he sees around him.

If a (much) less well-off person dreams of high living, then it is a dire symptom of self-satisfaction, and not a good omen for anyone hoping to succeed in an endeavour. Beware of a dream like this; it is a sign that you need to review your attitude to work, wealth and success. However, if you dream that you are receiving money in return for exercising your talent, then you have a realistic and hopeful outlook, and you are likely to succeed in what you are doing.

The dream world abounds in ambivalences such as these. An old person can symbolise wisdom and understanding, but also impending decrepitude and death. The exact meaning of the dream depends upon the mix of other images and symbols. For example, if you dream you are in a forest and see a lion lying asleep on the other side of a stream, it could be that your dream is telling you that you have vital powers (the lion) that have yet to be awakened (sleeping). You have to cross the water to wake him up, which is an indication of the ease or difficulty with which you do this. If you have identified "water" as an archetype of an obstacle or barrier, then you may have to strive harder for self-realisation – but this is no reason *not* to do it. The dream is merely telling you what is possible and dreaming is always an indication of what is definitely within reach.

BLUEPRINT FOR ANALYSIS

There is no such a thing as a typical dream, but when you are analysing one, the following set of questions will apply to the majority of them, questions that will help you arrive at an understanding of the dream, outside of any specific meanings that the symbols may have. These are the more obvious questions to ask:

- Who is in the dream?
- What is in the dream?
- What happens in the dream?
- How do you feel in the dream?
- If the dream is about an everyday situation, do you see anything out of place?
- If the dream is about a bizarre situation, do you recognize anything familiar?
- Where are you in the dream, an active participant in the drama or a spectator?
- If you are "only watching", did you want to be involved – or vice versa?

With these details in place, you are now ready to name the dream.

NAMING DREAMS

In my section on dream capture, I advise readers to name each dream as you write it down. This is because every dream is unique, with its own identity and message. Naming a dream so that it stands out in memory is a good way to refer swiftly to it when you are comparing its events with another dream. However, in your search for the "right" name, do not become too weighed down. We are all acquainted with Juliet's aphorism on the philosophy of naming things:

> "That which we call a rose/ By any other name would smell
> as sweet…" (Romeo and Juliet, 2:2:43-44)

Like many experienced writers, I have lost count of the occasions that an elusive title of an article has simply floated by magic – not too strong a word here – from a finished or nearly-so text. The older I grow, the less time I spend in brow-knit torture, because the synthetic process itself has grown a habit of delivering to my consciousness the name, which is why I advocate again and again to dreamers practise at the creation of name tags to accompany *every* recorded dream. To illustrate what I mean, consider the following experience. Some years ago, I dreamed that I was in an office setting, dressed in a respectable workaday suit and carrying an appropriate briefcase. I opened the briefcase and watched, horror-stricken, as a dead corvid fell out. I reeled in disgust at the sight of its dark feathers falling all over the pristine corporate flooring and wondered what effect the spectacle was having upon my colleagues. Upset, I awoke and struggled to pen the distasteful details in my bedside jotter. While writing, the phrase "bye-bye blackbird" floated into my head – light bulb! The dream corvid may have been a crow or a raven, but it did not matter; ornithological accuracy is not at stake here. Essentially, the dream was telling me to say "bye-bye" to my dead corporate – corvid – career, a message that I eventually drew profit from. To extract maximum benefit from the process, try to find the title of the dream as swiftly as possible after writing down its details. Remember, dreams are a form of currency that devalues with time, and the sooner teased out and put into use by you, the more beneficial for you.

WHEN NOT TO SHARE YOUR DREAM

Before you embark on your odyssey of self-understanding, I strongly advise you against telling anyone what you are doing. Anyone does not mean everyone, of course, and the luckier amongst you will know at least one person whom you trust and who understands you greatly. If you know someone like this, perhaps you can form a kind of partnership, helping each other with dream-interpretation and self-realisation? Otherwise, silence is the golden rule. People who lack imagination might dismiss you as slightly lunatic and at the same time, there are too many downright jealous people out there who, having neglected their own self-development, are ready to pour scorn on anyone who tries to live a more fulfilling life. Even well-meaning friends may see you as self-indulgent, tinkering around with esoteric matters when you ought to be getting on with the "real" world.

And I stress once more, the importance of *not* revealing the content of a dream to another party, until you have interpreted it and gained from it, to your satisfaction. Many years ago, a friend of mine undertook a temporary work stint among people she barely knew. One day, she told colleague 1, whom she had hitherto trusted, of a strange dream she'd just had about mutual colleague 2. Immediately, colleague 1 strode boldly to colleague 2, and told of my friend's dream. Colleague 2 regarded my (mortified) friend warily following this incident, and my friend never trusted unfamiliar colleagues with anything intimate again – good thing the posting was a temporary one. At the time, I consoled my friend as best I could and even today, I feel her pain. Now that I know so much more about dreams and dreaming, my advice is: if in doubt, don't set it about.

A POSTCARD FROM THE SUBCONSCIOUS

Dreams are postcards, straight from your subconscious, telling you about *you*. I could have told colleague 2 that my friend's dream was not necessarily about *her*, that her appearance in the dream was most likely as the personification of my friend's anxiety about an unfamiliar working environment. But I doubt if this explanation would have made colleague 2 feel any better; few people would relish, I am certain, being a "personification" of someone else's angst!

And yes, I do give examples of my own dreams throughout this text, but I can do this because they are "spent" dreams, information that I have used and profited from – recollect what I have written above about dreams being a form of currency? Revealing your dreams at the wrong time to the wrong person – and you don't know who that might be – will only compromise you personally and deprive you of any benefit that you might have gained from private interpretation. Be aware that getting in touch with your own subconscious is not going to be an easy task; do you really want an untrained person – no matter how trustworthy – doing it for you? If you are still not convinced, consider the following allegory.

Think of the subconscious as a closet filled with odds and ends, which can tell you much about your life, past and present. In the dreaming process, the subconscious is telling you which areas of life you should focus on now, to build a better future, the postcards I refer to. Very few outsiders, if any, can interpret this information accurately. And it works in both directions.

Supposing another person's subconscious *was* an actual closet that you could look inside. You could tell much about their life by looking at photograph albums and such, but you would interpret many details wrongly. The presence of a gun could mean the person enjoys hunting trips or has an interest in antique firearms. A stuffed bird could mean the person likes taxidermy or is trying to hide an embarrassing wedding present – or is a stand-in for Norman Bates! Without knowing the person, you never really *will* know. And even if you do encounter someone who does "get it", how many people would you really want nosing into your intimate life? Would you want strangers – or even people you know – pouring over details about you?

So, when *can* you talk about a dream? As I explained above, think of a dream as expendable currency; when you have gotten whatever value out of it, solved your problem or achieved whatever goal, then it is OK to talk about this wonderful, nighttime powerhouse. It all presses the point: when in doubt, stay silent.

BIG DREAMS, LITTLE DREAMS

The worst mistake the dreamer can make is to record only those dreams that sing in the memory long after they have taken place; you know the ones I mean, wonderful oneiric experiences of dancing with a rock star or of diving off a cliff and gliding towards a deep, blue sea. Sure, these BIG dreams are fabulous to experience but concentration only on the interpretation of these will leave gaps in the *total* picture of your psyche – and it is the bigger picture that you are after here. I liken big dreams to blockbuster movies, filled with memorable characters and riveting events, events that everyone talks about for years afterwards. I liken the "little" dreams, the fragmented images, whispered sounds and half-glimpsed words that are tied together by feelings rather than events, to topical news bulletins, weather forecasts and documentaries, in short, the information about what is really happening out there. Just think of what life would be like if you got your information *only* from blockbuster movies?

And be aware that "little" here does not mean unimportant; the storeowner, who listens only to the complaints of one, big socially elevated customer while ignoring the concerns of the multitude of workaday customers, is headed for trouble. That is why I constantly stress the importance of recording *every* dream memory. When you do this over a period of time, you see patterns emerging, dream themes and archetypes recurring. Another point is that using material gained in dreams to access the subconscious mind in order to sort out the thorny and difficult questions that have no apparent answer, leaves our wide-awake brain free to complete essential logical and material everyday tasks.

But enough – for now – of this and that. We are finally embarking on a fascinating voyage into the world of dream imagery. And just as children belong in families, I have grouped similar and related dream symbols into definite family groups.

The Concrete World

The material world is all around us; we live and breathe and walk and talk in it. We wake up every morning in a house or flat, work all day in an office or factory, school or hospital, and rest in the evening. We read books, watch movies, listen to music – in short, enjoy works of culture that would not be in existence without the organisation and planning of other people. The house you live in, the clothes you wear, the food you eat; all are brought to you by the organised effort of other people. It is unsurprising then, that the majority of dreams are about the *concrete* world, the world of homes, hospitals and schools. And just as we identify people by their occupations, the dream people we encounter tend to have identifiable occupations. Actual places of work I have placed in my chapter **Journeys, Energy and Travel**; in this section, I focus upon the places where we live and interact with other people.

THE DREAM DWELLINGS

What with their anthropomorphic references, houses are obvious dream metaphors; windows as "eyes", the door as a "mouth", and so on. When referring to their "dream house", most people have in mind the house that they would/will build, when their financial ship sails into port. In dreams, buildings are metaphorical, expressing our hopes, fears and aspirations. Because of the legacy of our western architecture, certain building types are associated with particular social and commercial activities. These associations channel into our subconscious and express themselves in dream imagery. In her book, *The Dream Whisperer*, Davina

MacKail describes houses as "symbols of the psyche".[37] Over time, I have analysed and established archetypes for the most frequently appearing dream dwellings. I have had many dreams involving buildings and dwellings of all kinds: grand mansions, dilapidated houses and sleek, ultramodern apartments. When establishing these archetypes in your own dreams, bear in mind that the images you see will be influenced by the dwellings you have lived in, especially the ones that you have grown up in. The area you are in (attic, ground floor, basement?) makes dream buildings and building dreams even more complex and fascinating.

NEW HOUSES AND OLD HOUSES

I spent my youth in a bland, suburban house that had country cottage pretensions. When out and about, the adults that surrounded me showed frequent signs of hostility to the kind of exciting, ultramodern architecture that I loved, and still do love. Nowadays, when an ultramodern building appears in one of my dreams, it indicates my belief that I am not getting my just desserts in a situation, especially of the work and money kind. This is because while a child, the adults I knew rejected their – and my – modern heritage and clung to traditional buildings and ideas. Of course, your archetype of desire might be an old, grand house. In my dreams, grand houses stand for possibilities, with the many rooms and the ghosts of the many people that have lived in them. Dilapidated houses, whether old or new, are another matter. I have never dreamed of being in a ramshackle building without attendant feelings of fear, worry or regret. These buildings are the archetypes of situations that I want to get away from.

A PERSONAL EXPERIENCE

In a dream, I am with a group of people, going around an *old house*. It is dark but I am not afraid, because the darkness is lit with muted patterns

37   McKail, *The Dream Whisperer*, p. 102.

of glowing colour. There are various cultural activities in the different rooms, but I am looking for the loo. I go into one room, with a map on the table. I am still wondering where the loo is, when a woman comes in and speaks to me in a stern voice. The dream is telling me that I should look for more cultural activity, and not get *bogged down* in everyday details, i.e., the loo. The young woman is really a cultural priestess, and the map a guide to the future – if only I could have seen what was upon it. But no matter; it is many years since I have had that dream and put the advice it contained into action, which is why I am doing what I am doing today.

TWO WOMEN, TWO STORIES

Another curious dream occurred a number of years ago, just as my copywriting career was beginning, I dreamt about two women in an old house, one younger and one older. It was an odd building with the side wall missing, like an opened dolls' house, and I had a superb, cross-section view. On the ground floor, the younger woman was on her knees, as if supplicating something. The older woman was also on her knees, but she was in a room on the upper storey, filled with light that was pouring in through a window or hole in the roof.

Davina McKail has written that, in dreams, the basement of a house represents the unconscious and the past.[38] Ground-floor rooms represent the unconscious and everyday matters, while the bedroom stands for the intimate, inner self. The attic stands for both the higher self and the future. My dream was actually presenting me with an image of me in a state of becoming. The two women were actually the same person – me – at different career stages, one current and one projected. The younger woman is "doing OK" in her conscious everyday, mode but she is also seeking something better, i.e., on her knees. The older

---

38   McKail, *The Dream Whisperer*, p. 172.

woman has risen to something better, but she is also seeking the rewards that come with a higher, as in more developed, life.

FURNITURE, TABLES AND CHAIRS

The majority of us cannot get through a normal day without encountering a variety of tables and chairs, couches and armchairs, and people who live alone will have at least, the constant companionship of their furniture. In our speech, we refer to furniture in anthropomorphic terms, the *arms* of the chair, the *legs* of the table, the *face* of the clock. No wonder then, that furniture fills our dreams, as much as it does our homes!

Because of its anthropomorphic associations, dreams of furniture lend themselves to the methodology of Gestalt analysis. Talk to your table or chair; ask it why it is there and what its significance in your life might be. When recalling your dream, make note of everything significant about the furniture that you encountered: plain or fancy, modern or old-fashioned, decrepit or in working order? Was the item unoccupied or in use by you or someone else – perhaps you *were* the piece of furniture? It could be that you do not want to be "sat upon", like the chair, or "overloaded" like the table, or brushed aside, like the doormat? Gestalt-type conversations with items of furniture may help you plan a route out of a menial occupation and aim for a more fulfilling occupation.

IN BED WITH YOUR DREAMS

We do most of our dreaming in bed, so it's hardly a wonder when we dream about being in bed. The bed is the dream archetype of the beginning and the end of things, the place where you are born and you die. It is a place to experience love and pain, to recover from illness and to give birth. Another bed archetype is the uterus, a place where ideas are forged and nursed while you gather the energy to put them into action. At a physical level, it is a place of darkness where the frighteningly named "sleep paralysis" gives rise to oneiric hobgoblins, exemplified in Henri Fuseli's painting, *The Nightmare*. Those of you who have seen the painting know that it is of a young woman, lying asleep on a couch or bed, surrounded by strange, nocturnal creatures, supposedly part of her nightmare. Incidentally, whenever I encounter a bedside hobgoblin, I have a way of dealing with it that means that I am never afraid – but more about this topic in my chapter **Sleep Disorders and Nightmares**.

CLOTHING

Since we wear clothing every day, it is not surprising that items of clothing are imbued with profound meaning in dreams – and it is not for nothing that "habit" is another word for a garment. If, in your dream, you see yourself dressed in a familiar garment, your subconscious could be asking you to consider changing what you do, every day. Of course, much of your dream's meaning will depend on how you feel throughout; happy or sad, worried or hopeful. Surprisingly, it is a good omen to wear old and worn clothing in a dream, particularly if you are embarking on a new venture. What is not such good news is the experience of wearing new and elegant clothing. For the majority, this is a warning from the subconscious against a new undertaking at the time. If you are wearing an unfamiliar and remarkable garment, such as an extravagant hat, use the Gestalt method – which I describe in **Meditative Exercises** – to converse with the hat and to find out how it may fit into your life. In your dream, if you lose a favoured article and don't find it again, then ask your subconscious to return it – the answer might surprise you.

BOOKS

Books are the repositories of all of the knowledge in this world, the writing of which quite often originates in the dreaming process itself, a fact that I constantly refer to, throughout this text. The meaning of a dream surrounding a text will depend upon the condition of the book old and battered or new and shiny?, on whether or not you recognise the author, and of how the book fits into the wider circumstance of the dream:

- Is the book on its own or do you see it with other books?
- Are you reading the book in unison with a college class?
- If so, are you a student or a teacher?
- Are you reading alone?
- In a fertile and idyllic setting or a derelict wasteland?
- Is the text obscure or transparent?
- Is the text technical, creative, romantic – and so on?

If you cannot read the book because the text is blurred or the pages will not open, it could be your subconscious telling you to look more closely at what seems like a familiar situation.

MIRRORS

From Alfred Lord Tennyson's famous narrative poem, *The Lady of Shallot*. I quote:

> "And moving thro' a mirror clear/ That hangs before her all the year,/ Shadows of the world appear./ There she sees the highway near/ Winding down to Camelot:"

The poet may have written his narrative in 1842, but he seems to have exercised a curious prescience in the matter of social media. Because what else are our computer and television and telephone screens but highly technological mirrors presenting us with shadows and images of a world that is not immediately in front of us? And actual mirrors are so ubiquitous in our times, that we are unaware that it has not always been thus. The first mirror in literature was most certainly the pond that Narcissus gazed into, enthralled by his own reflection, an activity that eventually turned him into the flower of the same name. For centuries, only shamans gazed into rare and precious mirrors, carrying the act of "scrying", that is, looking for images of the future and information from on high, in their dim surfaces. *Snow White* and *Beauty and the Beast* are only two fairy tales featuring magic mirrors. By the sixteenth century, mirrors were still a rarity, held in possession only by the upper classes. But our self-awareness was growing and in Shakespeare's play, *King Richard the Second*, we see the monarch contemplating himself in a glass:

"O flatt'ring glass, Like to my followers in prosperity, Thou dost beguile me." (4:1:279-281)

When he wrote this scene, Shakespeare was most likely aware of the superstition surrounding the mirror. Associated with magic and sorcery, the mirror would have been a bringer of bad luck, and the scene with the mirror is a pointer to the monarch's eventual usurping by Henry IV. For this reason, pay great attention to how the mirror appears in your dream. A broken mirror may be telling you to consider your future plans carefully. If you see your reflection, you will almost certainly look a little – or even a lot – different to how you do in reality. Try to remember what details are changed and what the symbolism is indicating. For instance, a larger than normal mouth could be a warning from your subconscious that you are speaking too freely about an important matter. Seeing another person you know could indicate that they are about to become significant in your life. And if that person has features altered, for instance, larger than normal ears, it could be a warning from your subconscious that he or she has vital knowledge to impart to you.

The World of Work

COMMERCIAL BUILDINGS

Buildings in which much commercial activity takes place, like banks and business headquarters, have often been built in the classical style, that is, with porticoed entrances and Georgian windows, carved friezes and string coursings. These references exude an aura of permanency and stability, important when imparting confidence to customers and trading partners. If your dream features a building like this, it is possibly a sign that you are confident about the future or have a very secure present.

Not everyone likes classical certainties, however. Medieval building references became fashionable during Victorian times, with castellated parapets, turrets and tall, narrow windows placed irregularly on the facades of domestic dwellings. The Victorian personality fancied a hint of the unexpected and the arcane – who knew what secrets lay hidden behind that turret window? To see a medieval building in a dream could mean that an exciting or unexpected event is about to take place – a lottery win, a new romance or maybe a turn of fortune in business?

Purpose-built schools, hospitals and factories tend to be "modernistic" and devoid of ornament. In addition, buildings with shining glass and metal facades tend to house new, high-tech and dotcom-based businesses, in contrast to the premises of traditional banking and commodity-trading establishments. If you see a modernist building in a dream, it could mean that you need something new in your life, possibly taking a novel approach to an omnipresent situation. Once more, the meaning of your dream building will depend on the accompanying imagery. For instance, if your classical building is on fire, it could be warning you not to take security or certainty for granted. Or if that deliciously spooky medieval house contains only the people and things you know and love, it may be a sign that you need not expect anything new to happen for a long time in your life. Or if that shining, modern edifice pulls back to reveal a maggot-stuffed corpse – well, that's for *you* to figure out.

CLEAN DREAMS AND GRAND SCHEMES

The metaphors of domestic cleaning are fairly obvious; take one stale, grimy and untidy house. Add one reluctant householder, a bucket, mop and tin of elbow grease. Add a dash of energy, mix and – woosh! The result is a shiny, sparkly, clean interior, all ready for starting anew, making a good and fresh beginning in any endeavour – work, love, family relations or whatever is significant in your life. As I pointed out in my chapter, **The Concrete World**, a dream house is often a symbol of the self, and the act of cleaning it could contain an important message for you, a warning to pay attention to a particular area of your life. Dream of cleaning windows and your subconscious could be nudging you to maintain a clear vision in an important matter or examine a situation more closely before making a significant move. Cleaning a door, doorway or doorstep could be telling you to curb your impulsive speech or, since doors work both ways, to pay more attention to the speech of others.

A dream of mopping the floor or cleaning the basement of a house could be a subconscious dictum to get it right from the ground upwards, "it" being the establishing of something significant in your life – or to postpone a new project until you have "cleaned up" an established project. As with all dreams, much of the meaning of your oneiric rubbing and scrubbing will stem from other details in the dream. Is the house old or new? Is it a house that you own or live in – or does it belong to someone else – or is it a fantasy house? Are you alone or are other people with you? Is the interior simple or elaborate, dark and muted or bright and filled with lightness? Is everything in working order, or in a state of dilapidation? As ever, only you can interpret your own dream – but for most people, the majority of clean dreams occur before embarking on grand schemes.

THE OFFICE

So many types of office exist, and so many divisions of labour are present within its confines, that a dream involving *the office* is just as likely to be about relationships and life in general, than actual work. See my chapter, **People and Relationships**, for more on this topic. If you do experience an office dream, which you feel definitely *is* about work, what post do you occupy? Are you in charge of the situation or engaged upon a menial task? Do you feel competent or are you out of your depth? Are you alone or with colleagues and – how do you feel – happy, sad, scared, isolated or insecure?

MODERN TIMES: THE FACTORY

Factories are marvellous places, pumping out everything our hearts desire, day in, day out. The modern factory evolved during the industrial revolution. Initially, they were dark and dangerous places where many lives were maimed or even, lost, as they made money so that an elite could lead privileged lives. Matters have improved since then, but our atavistic fears surrounding the "dark, satanic mills" remain; witness Charlie Chaplin in his movie, *Modern Times*, in which a character becomes quite literally caught up in the machinery that he is operating.

The entire incident is a metaphor of the alienation of large numbers of people who feel that places of work, institutions and organisations have taken over their lives. When analysing your factory dream, ask the usual questions about your status, role, feelings and so forth, in the total picture. And do not neglect to ask: *what is the factory producing?* Perhaps *you* are the product here, reacting in the same way to a situation, every time, even when a situation warrants a change of attitude?

DOWN ON THE FARM

By and large, the wilderness and wild animals stand for the untamed within us, untapped powers and resources that we possess but most often, that we do not use effectively. As they belong to the organized world, farms, cultivation and domesticated animals bear slightly different connotations. Much of our household produce has its origin on the farm: meat, milk, butter, cream, eggs, wool and leather. Because we have contained and controlled farm livestock over aeons, these beasts are considered less intelligent and more docile than their wilder cousins. For this reason, we forget that farm animals are not ubiquitous, but are actually quite rarefied: in all of the thousands of years of domestic farming, man has succeeded in subduing only a handful of species – cow, sheep, goat, pig, horse, dog, cat, and a few species of fowl….this list is *not* endless.

When you encounter a farm animal in a dream, question what qualities it embodies. For example, a cart horse might stand for patient strength, the cow provides a bounty of milk and butter and so on, and the sheep, because of its woolly coat and habitual huddling with other members of its herd, warmth and sociability. Be aware that a racehorse is a very different animal from its cart-drawing cousin, and that what we *believe* to be true about a species is more significant than agricultural accuracy. Questions to ask include: are you the farmer, or a labourer or a stranger on the farm? Consider whether you were *with* the animal or if you *were* the animal? Are you together or penned separately? Was the animal ignoring you or trying to communicate something?

A talking horse might be telling you to begin thinking outside of your (horse) box, to try taking a course of action that you may not have considered before, while a cow providing coloured milk might be forewarning you of unexpected results in a cherished endeavour. An arable farm is one where crops are mainly grown, which is a metaphor of fertility aside from dreams of a green wilderness. Unlike the plants of the wilderness, we have a modicum of control over cultivated vegetables, fruit and flowers, though not entirely. Dreams of a flourishing field could indicate that your long-laid plants are about to bear fruit. When analysing your arable dream, question whether a particular plant is significant, or is in any way out of the ordinary. For example, encountering a field of giant carrots could be a sign that matters that you thought were in place are about to get out of hand. Gardens are closely related to arable farms; remember that glorious patch of talking flowers in Lewis Carroll's book, *Alice Through the Looking Glass?*

Try to identify the flowers that you see growing and question if the blossoms have an underlying meaning for you, outside of the accepted conventions of say, forget-me-not. For instance, a former lover may have given you say, a bunch of pink roses; if you see similar flowers growing, it could be a signal to get back in touch. However, dying or dead flowers could signal the end of the relationship. Look for other details: is the garden enclosed? Does it have a fishpond, dove cote, beehive, greenhouse, maze, seating area, lovers' bower, fountain or sundial? Are you alone, or with other people?

SCHOOL DREAMS AND SEATS OF LEARNING

Dream archetypes for schools include: a place of multiple possibilities, personalities and experiences, a place of discipline and hard work and (very much so for me), a place where I did not always want to be. A few years ago, I experienced an entire spate of school dreams, all quite different and many of them bizarre. In one dream, a person with whom I was at school gave me the gift of a sizeable voucher, which could only be spent on a piece of obsolete technology. I awoke, filled with disappointment – and realised that that was the way I had always felt about that particular seat of learning, i.e., I had taken away a shed load of skills that had become obsolete. At one level, this dream was a warning to keep on developing, to think outside the box and take new approaches, else risk becoming a backwater. Here, be aware that the archetype of teacher is, on the surface, quite apparent: a leader, guru, sage, tutor, and so on. However, this should not prevent your searching for your own, more subtle archetypes. After a series of dreams that spanned years, I did eventually make the leap from pupil to working in a classroom.

HOSPITALS AND HEALING

The standard dream dictionary meaning of a hospital is that it serves as a warning to the dreamer to alter his or her way of life, because of a risk to health or fortune. I concur with this, but the dream will not make much sense unless you analyse the remaining imagery. Questions to ask when you dream about a hospital or other place of healing include: where are you in the dream?

• What are your surroundings; are they typical of a medical clinic?
• Who is with you; people that you recognise or are you in the company of strangers?
• Are you a patient, a visitor or a medic?
• Are you in a position of power or are you prone?
• If you are a patient, what part of your anatomy is afflicted and what treatment, if any, are you offered?
• How happy are you with the proceedings and what other emotions are you experiencing?

A PERSONAL EXPERIENCE

In one dream, I was lying in a hospital bed, when a friend of mine arrived. Suddenly, I put on a coat over my hospital gown and left the place, got into a red car with a man I did not know and left my handbag behind. In reality, this would be a highly questionable and dangerous situation and in the dream, I knew this – yet, I did it. My feeling of worry became so overwhelming that I awoke before anything "bad" could happen. Just months after this dream, I embarked on a creative project with a person I did not know. Such was my longing for novelty that I ignored the warning signals in my head (*the red car*) and launched right into the work. Not long afterwards, my role in the project ended abruptly and unhappily. If I had paid heed to the symbols in the dream, I could have worked out it was a warning against taking a role before being quite ready for it. In the dream, I was prone (*lying in bed*) when my friend arrived.

In reality, this friend is also working at writing and she is the archetype of *creative development*. I pulled the coat on over my hospital clothes (*unready to leave*) and left without my handbag (*creative faculties*). My archetype for the hospital in dreams includes *a place I do not want to be but where I might need to be*. Curiously, because hospitals tend to be filled with people who have knowledge at many levels and in many disciplines, the hospital is also *a place of learning*. Push the envelope further and you may find that learning is actually a kind of *healing*. I was not prepared to go through this healing and suffered because I left the place prematurely. Would I have taken the creative job if I had understood the warning in the dream? Possibly, but the consequences of my action would have reinforced the significant message of the dream and having had the experience once, I have learned a lesson. So, analyse hospital and medical dreams as thoroughly as you do the others. Remember that actual healing can apply to your career, love life or a relationship with one of the family.

The Natural World

A dream of the natural world is almost always a sign that you are doing something right, that you are about to realise a particular goal. In a dream, the colour *green* stands for growth and fertility, as do green trees and abundant grass and other kinds of greenery.

In literature, the "green" world has ever been the place of magical happenings. We see this in Shakespeare's plays, such as *A Midsummer Night's Dream* and *As You Like It*, where characters move out of the everyday world into a disordered realm where anything is possible. In this natural world, relationships are reordered, alliances are forged and conflicts resolved, before the characters return to the normal, more pedestrian world. Much of literature feeds into the idea that the unhappy personality is healed in natural surroundings. This recurrence of the landscape is almost universal in the Gothic narrative; the action always takes place in a "far away" setting, almost as in a fairy tale. In *Romance of the Forest*, by Ann Radcliffe, practically all of the action takes place against a backdrop of landscape. Early in the narrative, heroine Adeline falls into a fever immediately following her rescue from the brigand's house by the La Motte family, where her supposed father has dumped her. Adeline recovers her faculties by rapt gazing at vistas of natural beauty:

> "The fresh breeze of the morning animated the spirits of Adeline, whose mind was delicately sensible to the beauties of nature."

But in spite of the beauty of the landscape, it also contains danger.

European folk literature is chock with tales like *Hansel and Gretel* and *Little Red Riding Hood,* of children lost in forests, of marauding bears and wolves, and of nobility imprisoned in ivy-covered castles. These tales remind us that dense forest once covered the continent, and that venturing even a few hundred yards between the trees was fraught with danger. On a practical level, the forest is shelter from the cold in winter, the heat of summer, and a store of food for a myriad plants and animals. The forest is a symbol of the holism of life, a metaphor of growth and decay, death and rebirth.

In dreams, the forest is the archetype of *cycles of nature,* that is, the blending of spring into summer, followed by autumn into winter. Just as these cycles are inevitable, so are the consequences of the actions that we take. Another archetype is that of the puzzle. We say of a confused person that "he cannot see the wood for the trees". The forest is a reminder that the most momentous happenings in life have covert beginnings, for instance, the pregnancy that precedes a birth, the planning that goes into a work of art. What else is the flowering of the forest, only the glorious ephemera of deeper causes?

PERSONAL EXPERIENCE

When my copywriting career was taking off, I dreamed that I was walking along a country road. I crossed it and a white or silver car swerved to avoid me. This happened once more and I wondered if the driver(s) were being kind to me – or just preserving themselves? The road ended and I came to a grassy area criss-crossed by streams and shaded by trees. A wonderful light filtered through the trees, dappling everything mauve and green. Suddenly, I felt very happy and I whipped out my (dream) camera, wanting to capture the scene.

On analysis, I was on the road, the route to everything I wanted. The cars, representing fast-moving energy and riches (the silver), were actually trying to stop for me; *it was I who was avoiding them.* The wooded area represented my own life. The *trees are rooted, stubborn and conservative,* and the *streams are stagnant.* The dream was a warning that, in spite of my success, to be careful not to accept other people's terms and conditions too easily, else I stood in danger of avoiding the higher income and better success that could be mine.

WISH YOU WERE HERE: SEA AND BEACHES

Shakespeare's play, *The Tempest* has a coastal setting rather than a country location, the island being the magical realm of Prospero, the magus, of the monster Caliban and the spirit Ariel – the stuff that dreams are made on, indeed. Since the sea and the beach are places of shifting fortunes, it is unsurprising that many authors draw upon maritime imagery when creating book titles, e.g., *The Waves* by Virginia Woolf and *The Sea* by John Banville.

My dreams are filled with images of the sea, of sand and beaches. The beach is a place between sea and terra firma, caught between constant flux of the tides and rock-solid certainty of land. The beach is made of sand, a material used in construction. In general, sand in a dream – and in particular, the beach variety – stands for a state of flux, a myriad possibilities, since sand is fine, crumbly stuff before it is moulded and stiffened into more permanent forms. The beach is where the tide turns, where people relax and let go of everyday matters. With its roiling waters' edge, the beach symbolises changing fortune. Unless "fixed", as in cement, it will continue to morph and shift. In short, the beach is the archetype of *uncertainty*.

By contrast, the sea is constantly changing and no process will fix it in place. When the sea is calm, it mirrors the sky, but a violent sea will not reflect anything. The colours of the sea, blue, green and purple, occur at the higher frequency end of the visible spectrum, denoting higher consciousness. The sea is the archetype of time, tide and eternity. It is a kind of Underworld, a repository of memories of the past and dreams of things to come. The deep ocean symbolises the primordial world, since it is where life originated. In this subaqueous workshop lie buried the blueprints of practically every territorial life-form, making the ocean a repository of *possibilities*. Since possibility and uncertainty go hand-in-hand, it is not always clear if a dream about the beach and the sea is an occasion for optimism – or the opposite.

For years, I experienced various dreams in which I was by the sea, on a beach or even, out on the ocean and looking back at the shore. Sometimes I felt happy and sometimes not but in all cases, I would awaken, filled with a wistfulness to get away from it all. In one instance, I dreamed of contemplating a row of cottages, built along a shoreline covered in grass. Following much observation, I noticed that the cottages situated along the grass margin were run-down to the point of dereliction, while the swankier and more desirable dwellings were situated upon the sand. The message of the dream was suddenly transparent, so obvious that I awoke immediately and sat up in bed, contemplating its implications. Should I choose a glamour-free path, endowed with fewer possibilities, on the safe and staid grass, or move daringly into a path of excitement and risk? To stress the poignancy and urgency of the options, the cottages stood against a backdrop of serene sea, green cliffs and a deep, blue sky, which you will see from my table of archetypes, stands for *optimism*. The dream was telling me that yes; I could play safe and be guaranteed, at least, a pleasant future. But greater rewards lay in store if I risked life "on the sand".

In another dream, I walked along a beach with a friend. It was a grey day and the beach was strewn with litter. As we approached the water's edge, the incoming tide threatened to overwhelm us. We ran back, only to be confronted by a cliff rising from the sand. I was about to climb the cliff when suddenly, my friend pulled me through a tunnel, and back to the same, grey landscape that we had just left. Cliff and tunnel are both archetypes of *access routes*. However, while digging a tunnel to a place might seem easier than climbing, it was not always the best route to take. The tunnelling subject lacks the air, light and clarity of vision of the climber. What is more, I was pulled back to where I started from by a friend who, though loyal and good, was the archetype of *unimaginative practicality*. The dream was not criticising my friend but advising me to be a little bolder and more imaginative in my own life, a matter that I have since remedied.

THE CAVE

In their book, *The Madwoman in the Attic*, Sandra Gilbert and Susan Gubar equate the image of the cave in literature with the womb from which we all come and the prevailing darkness with intuition. We see this in Greek mythology, where the Cumaean Sibyl, that female prophet, dwelt in a cave, as did Echo, the sad nymph whom Narcissus rejected in favour of his own image. Orpheus lamented Eurydice when she went to the underworld, when a snake bit her while she was collecting flowers. In his *Metamorphoses*, Ovid recounts how the sailors carrying Ulysses on his voyage enter the cave of Circe and are transformed into pigs when they accept the food and wine that she offers them. In fact, the cave represents the unknown, the dark space where everything begins and everything ends. And the cave plays a part in Plato's famous thought experiment, in which he likens the perception of mankind to the sights and impressions received by persons inside seeing shadows of the outside world cast upon its walls – a fine metaphor for the limited knowledge perceived by our accepted, five senses!

MY CAVE DREAM

My dreams of the cave have been few and far between, but I did have one dream in which I was wandering through a cave or caves, when I encountered three men, one fair, one dark and one with grey hair. Following consideration, I lay at the feet of the dark one. For a while, the feminist within me raged at this act of submission, until I explored the motifs a little, and realised that my action was one of choice, that is, no one forced me to "submit" in the situation. In choosing the dark (why dark?) man, my subconscious was indicating that I should consider exploring the unknown, pursuing career avenues that I hadn't yet considered. I accepted this advice, and it proved to be sound.

STORMS, RAIN AND SNOW

The clue to deciphering a rain-sodden dream depends much upon where it is falling, how heavy it is, and the effect upon the landscape. Gentle rain upon a green and fertile pasture indicates that your actions will lead to the good times, while a downpour upon a blasted heath has a less encouraging slant. Carefully question the direction in which your actions are leading you. A storm that clears before your dream ends is a sign that with effort, your difficulties will go away and a brighter future lies in store. In dreams, snow – the frigid mantle that obscures everything, is often indicative of underdeveloped skills and talents that, if put into use, might prove a route to your success. Once, I had a dream in which I walked along a country road. My brother, whom I have long identified as an archetype of unrealised dreams, was beside me. As we walked, we could see a snow-covered landscape, white, peaceful and beautiful. A few months later, I dreamed that a white van pulled up alongside of my home and six maids stepped out, all wearing white aprons. Before the end of that year, I had a dream almost identical to the first one, namely, that I was lying in a white room while recovering from a medical ordeal. As in the first dream, I was anticipating the future, when I heard a voice say: *learn to communicate, learn to communicate…*

There was no question of a radio or television broadcast interfering with my sleep, since I refuse to have these things in my bedroom. On analysis, I was in recovery (the hospital) from a traumatic career experience and I was wondering what to do next. The "can-do" feeling stemmed from my belief that life could and would get better. The appearance of my brother in the next dream was an indication that my career was about to spring into blossom after a long winter (the snow). The six maids in the next dream possibly represented the qualities that I needed to develop in order to reach my goals: talent, optimism, energy, ideas, skill and imagination. Interestingly, a maid in my dreams is the archetype of *can-do*, the emotion that I felt in the first dream. In the last dream, the voice telling me to *learn to communicate* was the missing link for success in my copywriting career, which began soon afterwards.

Of course, the exact meaning of a snowy dream depends upon where you live: in much of the world, the arrival of snow is not certain every year. When it does fall, it is a rare and lovely phenomenon, but it does not last long. In a dream, the arrival of snow could be warning you to be on the alert for a once-in-a-lifetime opportunity.

But alluring as it is, snow can also provoke danger for unguarded travellers, whether on foot or in a vehicle. Hans Andersen was aware of this when he wrote *The Snow Queen*, a tale in which a glittering and sexually-enticing woman lures away the prepubescent Kay from his young sweetheart, Gerda. When analysing your snow dream, consider carefully whether you are simply responding to an enticing exterior, whether a new lover or a job offer, and avoiding asking revealing questions.

FIRE POWER IN DREAMS....

Some years ago, I had an unsettling dream in which Britain was a no-go area, beset by hordes of virus-stricken, zombie-like people who would set fire to everything they touched. Terror-stricken, I barricaded me into my room and hid under the bedcovers, only to discover my mattress had begun to smoulder – you can guess that I awoke shaking from *that* one!

Fire has been in the news since the days of Prometheus. One of the four elements of the classical world, fire is a power with the potential for great benefits – and can wreak havoc in equal measure. Small wonder then, that London marked the anniversary of the Great Fire with a burning installation on the Thames - *not* surprising then, that fire breaks out occasionally in dreams. Fire symbolises many things, personal power, a brush with those on high, warmth and light, cleansing and purifying, in short, the chance to start all over again. When fire appears in your dream, consider what role you play, for example, are you the subject who began the conflagration?If you started the fire, the dream could be a warning that you are exercising your powers injudiciously during waking hours, possibly in a work situation? In the dream, if the fire is pursuing you, it could be a warning that you are not taking enough responsibility in certain areas. The same is true if you need rescuing from a fire. Whatever the situation, it could be time to step back and question what you are doing. So, how can you tell when you are getting it right? A few years ago, I dreamed that I was working as a fire investigator in a hotel – is there such a profession? Whether real or no, it was a glorious dream. Two or three policemen arrived at the hotel, and with my bunch of keys – *symbol of control* – I allowed them enter and ask questions of the guests – all signs that I was in control of the situation. Although I cannot remember the conclusion, I awoke, filled with the content that comes of knowing that one's life is on the right track.

AIR AND GUSTS OF WIND

Wind is constantly moving in streams around the Earth, an unseen force that is capable of great destruction. I have searched through my dreams yet; I have not found one occurrence of this force in my night-time adventures, which is rather a pity. Because in spite of its destructive capabilities, geologists have deduced that air currents and winds were one of the forces that spread life around the globe in pre-historic times, blowing seeds to its remotest corners and enabling many species to flourish.

A great force can knock you off of your feet – but it can also be a sign that good fortune is about to land you in a comfortable place. Whatever the context of your dream, prepare yourself for the success that is bound to come your way, throughout the waking hours.

DREAMTIME ANIMALS

The majority of us love to dream of an animal, especially if that beast is a beloved pet. All dreamers have experienced an anonymous creature or two, straying into their nocturnal visions. In certain cases, the animal is an emblem of someone you know during your waking hours; how often have you thought of someone as "foxy" or "a right cow"? However, in the majority of dreams, animals most often are metaphors of our links with the natural world. Animals embody our more feral traits; it is no accident that we often refer to our "animal instincts". Native Indian tribes were aware of this connection aeons before Charles Darwin published his *Origin of Species.* So-called primitive tribes constructed totems, charms and images of wild animals, which wearers believed would endow them with the better qualities of whatever beast; the courage of the lion, the strength of the bear, the swiftness of the wolf, and so on. It is no wonder that certain animals have particular meanings in dreams. When you experience a recurring dream of a particular animal, or even one glorious encounter with an exceptionally exotic beast, connect with the entity by getting into the meditative trance that I describe in my chapter, *Meditative Exercises.* Very broadly, relax deeply. While in this state, picture the beast and pull it into conversation. Ask questions like "who are you?", "what do you know that I don't?", "where will I go next?". Your answers may be surprising and enlightening.

PRINCESSES AND GOOSE GIRLS:
HORSE POWER IN DREAMS

Once upon a time, I was delighted to dream about a horse, not just an ordinary nag but one endowed with the power of speech. Before you readers descend into jokes about Mr Ed, be aware that a talking animal is a potent dream symbol. Humans are apt to be uber logical, using reason to work through our many conundrums. However, we have other skills and intuitions gained in earlier phases of biological and social development. Many of these skills have become buried under layers of sophistication and fallen into disuse. The appearance of an animal in a dream is often a message from the subconscious warning us that we are losing contact with our more atavistic instincts.

This is why the wise dreamer carefully archetypes oneiric animals as he or she does his or her other symbols and considers what message the subconscious is trying to send. The horse is a particularly potent symbol. From our earliest consciousness, the horse has been a mythical beast, featuring in the cave paintings of Lascaux. Of significance also are the ancient chalk hill carvings of horses, such as the one seen in Uffington, England. Although horses, like pigs, cannot fly, the ancient Greeks gave us Pegasus, the winged horse.

Eventually, I traced my own dream horse to Falada, an important presence in the fairy tale, *The Goose Girl*, by Jacob and Wilhelm Grimm. In the story, an ageing queen sends her young daughter to another kingdom, to be married. Despite being loaded with jewels and money, the daughter's only companions are her chambermaid and her talking horse, Falada.

On the journey, the chambermaid tricks the princess out of her fine clothes and assumes the royal mantle, herself. On arrival at the kingdom where the princess is to marry, the chambermaid has Falada slaughtered because she fears that he will tell the truth. However, the real princess rescues his head and has it nailed to the gate under which she goes daily to mind geese. But death fails to quieten Falada, who reminds the princess of her true identity, every day. Through various twists and turns, the identity of the "goose girl" is discovered and the usurper cast out. So, what can a talking horse teach us?

According to Bruno Bettelheim: *independence and transcending childhood require personality development, not becoming better at a particular task or battling external difficulties.*[39] The old queen knew what she was doing, sending her child out into the world, so apparently vulnerable. The young woman's true wealth was not her gold, but her own worth, in combination with the magic horse that daily reminded her of who she was. In our time, too many of us undersell ourselves, not setting high career goals and reaching out for the things we really want. Worse again, we often choose an attractive, easy-seeming route, not considering the options that it might close off, later on. My dream was telling me to use "horse sense", to become more intuitive about career moves. Even today, when I am confronted with a choice, I ask myself: do I want to be a princess or a goose girl? This has become such an important process that Falada has now joined my line-up of dream counsellors.

CATS, LIONS AND TIGERS

In my time, I have had precious few dreams concerning the adorable and fluffy, domestic cat – rather a pity, from my point of view! More common in my dream lexicon are nocturnal encounters with the larger, wilder members of the species, that is, tigers and lions. This is not a bad thing because, according to my dream dictionary, encounters with exotic animals indicate a connection with the extraordinary and the unusual, a foreshadowing of special events in life. And according to Davina MacKail in her book, *The Dream Whisperer*, this is indeed a gift, a sign

39   Bettelheim, *Uses of Enchantment*, p. 142.

that the dreamer is possessed of great intuition.[40] Once, I met and laughed with a cuddly lion, which had a "human" voice. The dream happened when I was going through a rough time, health-wise. On analysis, I did not find the dream had any particular meaning except to offer assurance and cause for optimism. In the longer term, all my medical tests were proved negative of dangerous disease. To that lion I say, "thank you".

Another time, I woke up, flush with the dream of a tiger. This was no cute'n'cuddly cartoon beast, like the one that came to tea, but a very tiger-ish tiger, all black-striped flaming fur and tensile whiskers, and jaws and claws in the right places. This tiger was not aggressive; I won't say he was tame or friendly, but he did not show interest in my companion and I as – ahem! – lunch guests. He just lay down, pressed his face against the window of the kitchen that Mum and I were inside of, and fell asleep. Tigers are solitary and territorial animals, symbols of wealth and sexual potency – and to see one asleep outside of my kitchen window was extraordinary. What is it about the feline species and why do cats occupy such a large space in our imaginations?

Throughout the ages, cats seem to have been either revered or reviled. This is possibly due to their untameable quality. Whereas the dog has always had a use as a faithful companion or a trusty worker or a combination thereof, the only function of the cat is to hunt mice, an instinct for which there is no training. Because of this unfathomable nature, the cat has ever had an aura of mystery about it. In ancient Egypt, this quality led to cat worship while in the European Middle Ages, the same quality led to associations of the cat with witchcraft, and countless felines were consigned to flames alongside their hapless, human owners. Now, I reckon that the wheel has spun once more and we positively laud the elegant, enigmatic animals – is it any wonder that

---

40   MacKail, *The Dream Whisperer*, 168-169.

a scientist named Schroedinger cast a notional cat into one of the most famous thought-experiments, ever? Not all cats are elusive and aloof, of course – think of cartoon characters such as Bagpuss or Top Cat. In one rare dream of a cat, I cuddled an uber-friendly, fluffy ginger-and-white number – aaah! – have you ever *not* wanted to wake up? In another dream, an unknown person presented me with newborn kitten from a litter – no, I was not about to become a mum. But the elusiveness of the situation – the unknown person – and the little bundle of mystery represented by kitten – indicated that something new and unexpected was about to begin in my life – and it did! The exact meaning of your dream depends on the entire play of details, of course.

If you have an exhilarating phantasm of chasing a cat or cat-like animal, then life could be telling you to follow a new idea or business venture. However, if the cat turns and scratches you, then beware of whom you trust and how you lay out your money. If you chase the animal without result, then life may be warning you that there are certain things you will never understand – again, context is all. Even the species can make a difference; matters to consider are whether your dream cat is of an exotic panther or do you dream of a kitty you actually know and love?

The most interesting point of my above dream is the tiger. It is significant that the tiger is not attacking me. The problem is my lack of communication with the tiger. I am afraid, even though the tiger is docile and sleepy. But then, the archetypal tiger is not like this, only potent and strong. Obviously, I would need to awaken the sleeping tiger, an action that – in reality – would carry great risk. The tiger might be aggressive or even dangerous, or simply might fail to provide the communication I want. In all cases, I have to take the risk to gain the power. The important thing to remember is this – the power *is* available, which is good news rather than otherwise. And I do need to communicate

with the tiger to find out how I might gain a measure of its potency –
lesson in life!

DREAMTIME CANINES: DOGGIES AND WOLVES

Unlike the aloof cat, the dog is a friendly and faithful animal – and just
guess what the beast stands for in dreams? Pleased to report, a former
family pet often wanders into my dreams, and I always awaken with a
warm and happy feeling. However, if your dream dog bites, then beware
of a colleague who might seem to be a friend, but….and then, watch
out for the more elusive animals that belong to the family of canines.

The wolf has ever occupied a special place in cultural consciousness.
Though not mythical in the sense that it exists as an actual animal, we
credit the wolf with qualities like intellect, power and strength, which
have mythic status in human society. Little wonder, then, that the notion
of the wolf has entered our language in many ways, both subtle and
overt. We *keep the wolf from the door* when we are worried about money
and *wolf* down food when we are hungry. Stories like *Three Little Pigs* and
Little Red Riding Hood stem from atavistic fears of the wolf as a voracious
beast, ready to gobble everyone in its path – no wonder parents regaled
naughty children with tales of the *big bad wolf*? In addition to being
homilies of caution against outside forces, such fables are a warning to
young children against depending too much upon one sense organ from
which to gain pleasure, in the majority of cases, the mouth – witness
those constant requests for sweeties and other goodies?

In accordance with the methodologies of Bruno Bettelheim, I
psyched another spin on the tale of *Little Red Riding Hood*. I did not see
the grandmother as a hapless victim of the wolf, anymore. Rather, she
comes across as a greedy, lazy woman who lies in bed all day, awaiting
the arrival of her supper, and putting the life of a young girl in peril. In
addition to warning young children of *stranger danger*, the fable could be
a disguised warning to the child to set higher aspirations for the self – or

else become dependent and helpless like the grandmother? The little pig who builds his house (career, relationships?) of strong stuff survives the onslaught of the wolf while his weaker siblings perish. Older readers might recognize hunger for food as appetite for other physical activity, while the organised intelligence represented by the wolf demonstrates that the pitfalls of excessive sensuality do not strike at random. Whatever the meaning, the wolf is a potent symbol in dreams.

Following years of waiting, the wolf finally appeared in a dream of mine. However, he was not the ravenous beast of myth, but a white, fluffy and frightened creature, who dropped in upon our Christmas feast – archetype of *plenty* – and went away without attacking my companions – *facets of my personality* – or I. He didn't even demand food – maybe I was doing something right? I woke up, almost disappointed. On reflection, the dream could have been indicating that I was – or am – conquering the less tameable elements in life, but I would like to have spoken with the wolf – maybe in another dream?

BUG DREAMS AND WHAT THEY MEAN

A few years ago, for a window of about 24 months, dreams about insects bugged me. Like a hapless picnic-maker with swarms of midges hovering overhead, I could find no respite from dreamtime bees and phantasmal ants. On occasions, I would awaken from one insect dream, fall asleep again and step right into another. In one dream, the friends I went to meet had all acquired wasps' heads. In another instance, a horde of stinging insects had filled my bathroom. In a dream-come-true-type of dream, I availed of an opportunity to see a favourite comedian on stage – and he turned into a giant, non-specific man insect in front of a horrified audience. I experienced numerous instances of swarms of moths flying out of my bed, and out from under my bed and devouring my carpet - yet, in spite of all the buzzing, munching and chirruping, I would awaken and find not so much as a biting flea in the vicinity – and thank heavens for that!

But what was going on? Like larger animals, individual insects embody the qualities that they carry outwardly. For example, bees are industrious and make wonderful, sweet honey – but they also carry a sting in the tail. The businessman who dreams about bees should read the small print on every important document before committing to a deal. My dream about the wasp heads was a warning to not take everything – indeed, anything – at face value.

Moths are animals that clean up the environment by eating feathers and animal fur, and my "moth man" dreams were reminding me to clear up old business before embarking upon anything new. Alas, I have never dreamed of the moth's more colourful cousin, the glamorous butterfly, which is called "psyche" or "soul" in Greek. Because of its connection with metamorphosis, the appearance of a butterfly in a dream can be the herald of important, often spiritual, changes. I have yet to fathom the meaning of the buzzing in the bathroom, but I will unravel it one day.

THE BIRDS

Aside from farmhouse fowls and the few tropical species that we unfortunately cage, the majority of avian species are wild. In art and mythology, particular meanings have attached to the various species of bird; for example, the peacock stands for eternity while a raven is often represented alongside a practitioner of the dark arts. As with all dream imagery, do not adhere too closely to cultural symbolism; question what meaning the bird has for *you* in the dream.

A dream of birds wheeling about a blue sky is often a reflection of our own longings and as with all dreams, the meaning lies in the details. Is the sky settled or do clouds loom on the horizon? Are the birds healthy and vivacious – or are they weak and ailing? The sight of a bird with a broken wing could be your subconscious indicating that someone close to you is in need of help – or maybe it is *you* that needs help? Beware: the sight of many injured birds is an example of the *absurd* in dreams (see **Glossary**), an indication that you could be nurturing too many wounded souls and that you need to attend more closely to your own needs. Dreams like this are often accompanied by a feeling of being overwhelmed.

A WARNING

As with every other dream, beware of *not* reading the symbols and metaphors of the natural world deeply enough. Just as with the forest itself, which is the archetype of *arcane* events, look for the less apparent symbolism. Record all the details of a "natural" dream. The mountain or river may look very beautiful, but would you actually want to go there? Try to remember what plants were growing; were they your favourites or flowers you disliked? And don't forget that the most beautiful roses are covered in thorns. Are the animals gentle or fierce, or is there a variety of beasts? Above all, what is your role in the dream, prone or powerful? Other landscapes include the cosmos, the moon and the stars, and violent phenomena like earthquakes and volcanoes.

Journeys, Travel and Energy

The idea of journeys, travel and energy always fill me with excitement because life is made up of movement and progression as much as stasis and rootedness. The second set of qualities are essential to stability and identity, the first set, to providing the energy and resource for professional growth and prosperity. Work and travel are qualities that provide this energy. The work we do is an arena for professional development and an engine for expanding our wealth, and travel to new places provides us with a number of enriching experiences, depending upon how our personalities respond to it all. From this point of view, it is unsurprising that work, travel and vehicles are frequent emblems for the majority of dreamers.

DREAM FOODS AND NIGHT-FARES

I have placed this section in this chapter because food, like money, is a form of energy, an enabler to carry out our chosen projects. It does not always make us "happy", but without it, we can do nothing. No wonder then, that dreams of food are among the most frequent that we experience – but just as we never devour the same meal twice, not all dream banquets are alike.

Nothing is so frustrating as those dreams in which you are seated in front of a table laid with a delicious meal that vanishes just as you are about to taste – or you simply wake up before you can do so. I have had many dream experiences like this and I have also been confronted by foods so disgusting (night-fares?) that waking up proved a pleasure. Desirable food is the archetype of the good things in life, of nutrition and wealth, information and society. In the majority of dreams, food symbolises a route to where you want to go. It can also serve as a warning. A few years ago, I dreamed that I was in an ultra-trendy restaurant, watching other people eat. Eventually, I collected a plate of tempting snacks but a *dark woman* in uniform said to me: *why do you think that those are not for you?* Deeply disappointed, I rejected the food, left the restaurant and wandered about town. On analysis, I found that the imagery stemmed from my own feelings of inadequacy. My rejection of the food was a symptom of my imagining that the good things of life were not for me, and the *dark woman* (archetype of *challenging*) was a facet of my own personality confronting me in this belief. In summary, the dream was warning me that feelings of inadequacy can drag a person into despondency and even, despair. The dream brought to mind all of the opportunities that I missed because I did not feel qualified or confident enough to reach out and grasp them, and a reminder to not make the same mistakes again. Try to build the total picture before jumping to conclusions about a person or situation in your dream.

THAT DREAM JOB

I've experienced so many different dreams about work and working, that it's as if I have been living a hundred lives and more. I've piloted planes, stood behind shop counters, driven cattle and nursed patients, among other occupations. I've even been an actress on a movie set – and no, I did not dash out and audition for RADA! For anyone seeking career guidance from dreams, these experiences are not necessarily a pointer to what you should be doing with your life. Aside from its not being possible or most likely, not appropriate to fulfil all of the callings that you are dreaming about, these images are more likely to be archetypes than vocational callings.

For example, a dream about piloting a plane or driving a vehicle may be a message from your subconscious indicating that you can or should *take more control* about certain important areas of your life. A dream about acting on a stage or film set may be a warning that you are trying too hard to fulfil *the many roles* that you assume in your waking hours, worker, father, husband, wife, mother and so on.

So, how do you know when your subconscious is trying to steer you in a definite, vocational direction? Many years ago, I had a dream that I was standing in an employment bureau. There was a man seated beside a typewriter, and I was telling him that I just had to find a job as a copywriter. I quote: 'it's my identity; it's who I am.' Immediately, I awoke with a strong sense of yearning that stayed with me all day, in fact, until I got my first copywriting assignment. It is the *earnestness* that you feel in a dream about a particular occupation, those feelings that you don't "laugh off" on awakening, that will point you in a definite direction.

PERSONAL EXPERIENCE

In a particular dream, I was working for an ex-boss, but not in familiar surroundings. He had transformed from a computer consultant into a fine-art dealer, selling paintings by Jacob Ruisdael (old boss, old *master*, get it?). In reality, at the time, I was experiencing "progression" problems with a new calling and I was considering returning to a former occupation. In the dream, I was quite content with my "old master" until a schoolteacher – indicated by her academic gown - whom I subsequently worked out to be my *dark woman* archetype, handed me a piece of paper with directions written upon it. Although I can't remember the exact words, I remember feeling suddenly very unhappy, overworked and underpaid. By now, I was aware that the *dark woman* archetype was warning me against taking a too-obvious course of action. The dream was a warning not to go backwards in time, not even for a job I had enjoyed – who wouldn't enjoy working with Old Masters? – or for a boss whom I had liked.

DREAMS OF WEALTH

Throughout the ages, ascetics and sages have declared that "money can't buy happiness" and they have found ways to survive without it. I bow to such ingenuity but the majority of you will have found – just as I have – that a healthy flow of cash is essential to live effectively in a world where money is the only form of exchange. Money oils the wheels of our lives, making it truly turn around. It is an enabler, giving us freedom *to have, to be* and *to do*. It is also a signifier of other forms of success. Sure, money can't buy happiness; it was never meant to; in its proper place, money keeps our lives mobile and prosperous, all the year round. It is no wonder that we all have dreams about money, mostly during our waking hours. We dream of money because we want more of it – or fear losing what we already have.

As with all other archetypes, the meaning of money and wealth in a dream is tied to the financial status of the dreamer. A prosperous person is likely just channelling his environment and spending habits into his dreaming hours. Wealth in the dream of a poor person can be an encouraging omen if the subject is actually earning his money. Unqualified wealth in a dream is more likely to be the archetype of unearned status or reward, something that the dreamer should be aware – and beware – of.

Far more useful are those dreams in which the dreamer receives an idea that, if put into action during waking hours, can lead to professional and financial success. That is why it is important to keep a dream diary, followed by thorough analysis. Go back through your roll of dreams. Read each one carefully and if you happen across one that makes your heart beat a little faster, then you may have the nub of a business or creative idea. If you feel – and feeling is important here - that the dream is unfinished and that you need more information, try to "finish" the dream using the techniques I outline in my chapter, **Meditative Exercises**.

TRAVEL IN DREAMS

When you record your dreams over a period of time, you will certainly notice recurring excursions to - or phantasms about - a particular country. If you have grown up or lived in another country or countries, such dreams are unsurprising. As ever, meaning and meanings lie in the archetype of whatever country, and its context to other events.

I grew up in Ireland and among its archetypes are *green* and *green-ness, youth, naivety* and *unready-ness*. However, green is also the archetype of *growth* and *fertility*, of an *abundance of possibilities* worth exploring. My dreams of the place often coincide with a project I am working on, a warning that my newly-fledged program may not be as ready for airing as I would wish. When not working on anything, a dream of Ireland is an admonition to go through my ideas' book in search of inspiration – an activity that never fails to lead to a fresh project.

Dreams of Germany, where I have also lived, indicate my longing to increase my skills, to go to a new place or to try something new. Dreaming of that country is also an indication of progress or even success in what I am currently doing. In one dream, I was in the job I did when I lived there, and my ex-boss was so pleased with me that we were eating pizza together. Although it was cold outside, I felt very warm and happy, a feeling that I woke up with. The dream was a sign that I had "arrived", and the pizza was a promise of even better things to come – which proved correct. To affirm this, I had a similar dream a few months later.

Overall, when you dream of a country, try to decipher how it relates to your life by using archetype analysis. For example, a dream of Italy could mean that you nurse a longing for *culture and good food*, while a dream of the US might mean that you are ripe for *adventure and new experiences*. Dreams of Spain may indicate a need for *rest, sunshine and wine* while phantasms of darkest Africa may be signposting you to explore *unknown areas of your personality*. Remember, it is what you believe about a country rather than what is true, is the route to revealing what your dream means to you.

DREAM VACATIONS

On browsing through my dream diary, the number of dreams on which I was on holiday, struck me. Indeed, certain of my musings read like a veritable Saga catalogue of mountain-top excursions, country house stopovers and endless (it seems) trips to the seaside. What is significant is that, in all of these dreams, I *knew* that I was on holiday. This held fast whether the location was familiar, unfamiliar or didn't involve sun, sea, sand or any of the usual vacation tropes. Holidays mean different things to different people. For a number of subjects, a holiday is simply an opportunity to gain rest and repose, either at home or at another location. For others, going on holiday involves foreign travel, hanging out in exotic locations and staying up much, much later than usual – whatever their definition of *wild living* happens to be. Whether quiet or crazy, the trope common to all holidays is escape; the act of getting away from what is pedestrian, everyday and commonplace.

ANOTHER POINT OF VIEW

In a weird way, all dreams are a sort of holiday, a mental excursion to places and points of view inaccessible during conscious hours. We think while we are awake, of course, but our thoughts are hidebound by convention and cultural habitude. This inhibition vanishes during dreams, resulting in the surprising and even shocking events that our waking selves could never imagine. In one holiday dream, I was in a resort that was amply furnished with beautiful swimming pools. I longed to go swimming (a favourite pursuit of mine) but for an unknown reason, I merely gazed longingly into the depths of the lovely, willow-patterned pools, and never dove into the water. Very swiftly, I transported to a dingy building where I picked up grubby coins – *filthy lucre* – from piles on the floor and then I woke up, bewildered and aching with frustration.

On analysis, the dream was warning me not to buy too much into the notion that only enjoyable activity (epitomised by the glamorous swimming pools) creates wealth. Sometimes, making profit means getting your hands dirty, the tale of the grubby coins. It was not a happy dream, but it proved to be a productive one, which is why it pays to uh, *pay attention to dreams*. And how you travel may be just as significant!

TIME HOPPING IN DREAMS

Just imagine being able to travel through time, to gain insights into history and to take a peek into the future, especially your own - imagine the world of power and wisdom at your fingertips. To travel through time has ever been a sci-fi fantasy, inspiring HG Wells to write the *Time Machine*, and Hollywood to make the *Back to the Future* movies. However, it is the one invention that has always evaded the ingenuity of real scientists. In spite of all of the technological marvels of the modern world, we still cannot scupper time. The conundrum is that we are bound to Earth's gravity and gravity is a distortion of time, keeping us on the 24/7 roller coaster. What do we do about this?

Oddly, we *do* scupper time; we do it every time we walk from one side of our living rooms to the others, and most journeys are generally longer than that. The physics are too complex to spin out here, but at every point on the globe it is a different time, at every moment of the day. Think, then, the power of getting onto an aeroplane and emerging on another continent and time zone, three hours later. Essentially, *all* travel is time travel; gravity is a weak force and we scupper it with every walk in the park – and there is another way to travel through time.

Like the majority of sleepers, I have experienced time travel in dreams. I have met and spoke with dead relatives. I have sat at the desks of the various schools and colleges that I have wandered through in my learning endeavours. I have dwelt in stone-age villages, medieval castles and in awe-inspiring futuristic environments. More than once, I have had that heady experience of being everywhere and in every time, all at once. Like Puck from *A Midsummer Night's Dream*, I have felt like shouting:

"I'll put a girdle about the earth in forty minutes"

on awakening. Maybe it was such a dream that inspired the Bard to write this immortal line?

When analysing a dream that has taken you to the past, look at all of its symbols carefully. First, listen to what your dead relatives are saying. According to your own databank of archetypes, are the symbols "good" or are they "bad"? What are your dead relatives telling you? Is the dream telling you to look to past experiences for guidance or to seek a solution elsewhere?

What can you learn from stone age/medieval/Renaissance society? Maybe that odd item or system you dreamed of is the key to your own future? The movement in the arts called surrealism took its time and space-hopping tropes from dream experiences. The word "surrealism" actually means "super realism", an indication that mind power underlies reality, not fantasy.

I point out in my chapter, **Dreams and Higher Perception**, that one belief common to all shamans is that of the non-linearity of time, which debunks all classical theories of chronology. With their theories of multi-verses and parallel universes, the quantum scientists are now on a level with shamanism. The shaman believes that the experiences of what we call the present are simply memories of the past and an anticipation of what will happen in the future.

OPEN SESAME: TECHNOLOGY IN DREAMS

Technology and dreams have always had a particular connection.

According to legend, Elias Howe patented the modern sewing machine following a dream about a tribe wielding spears that had holes just above the pointed tips. Long before our modern world of horseless carriages and machines that go up into the air, man wrote stories about flying carpets and doors that open to the subject's command. Indeed, one could say that modern technology is the direct *result* of men who had the courage to fashion ideas gotten in dreams into material form. Of course, it is not simply a question of experiencing a random dream about something fantastical and then creating it. Elias Howe had already been working upon the design of a mechanized stitching machine for a long time; following a spell of struggling with one, fiddly bit of the mechanism, his subconscious yielded to him the detail that his conscious mind could not supply.

Be aware though that there is very little of significance in a present-day person dreaming of technologies already in existence; my own dreams are filled with computers and televisions, planes, trains and automobiles. As with the majority of people, I am just channelling all of the stuff that we see all about us into dreams. As ever, the fun inherent in the interpretation of "techno" dreams lies in pinpointing the archetype of whatever piece of technology the dream involves. One curious discovery is that seemingly disparate technologies have similar archetypes. For example, take the fridge and the telephone, two superficially very different items of capability. But when you think about it, both the fridge and the telephone hum with life and use power. The phone is a work-enabler, a bringer of words and ideas, thoughts and conversation, while the fridge is a repository for food, the archetype of the *good things in life*, and of *energy*. Both the fridge and the phone are symbols of modernity, while the fridge has a light inside of it, a possible symbol of enlightenment.

What drew my attention to these parallels was a dream in which the workings of my fridge had somehow gotten entangled with that of my telephone. A couple of guys arrived to fix it, and they replaced my silver and grey fridge with a green and pale yellow fridge. The guys assured me that the replacement fridge was working perfectly and that insurance would cover the cost. As I put my food into it, I felt deeply disappointed that they couldn't fix my telephone. On analysis, the dream was a warning that, if I didn't take control of my life, others would do it for me, i.e., the two men replacing my fridge with a disappointing one. I have since worked out that grey (the colour of the fridge) is the archetype *of much intellectual activity,* which the men vanquished by taking away the fridge.

AWAY WITH THE FAIRIES

Every culture has its collection of supernatural little beings, its fairies and sylphs, sprites and elves, gnomes and leprechauns. Invariably, the creatures remain for the most part hidden, appearing to humans only during crises to deliver important communications or help finish vital tasks – no wonder that Santa's traditional helpers are elves! So entrenched is the notion of the hidden folk in our culture that, whether you believe that they exist or not, we should pay attention when we dream about them. In addition to being minute, fairies are often endowed with wings, giving them the power to move very quickly from one place to another. This quality gives them powers of communication, vital in days before the telegraph, telephone and eventually, the Internet. It is interesting that when the telegraph was invented, there was a massive surge of belief in these supernatural little beings, leading to the famous photographs of the Cottingley fairies.

In theatres all over Great Britain, fictional fairies flew over audiences on fly wings, a huge entertainment for patrons. In domestic households, newly installed electricity was known as the "household fairy", so swiftly did power help with the routine work. Whatever else happened, nineteenth-century technology did nothing to dispel belief in the little folk. It was as if our distant ancestors invented fairies in anticipation of a world with swift communications, mass transport and great assistance with manual labour. Overall, tiny supernatural people are the result of our atavistic longing for a better world – and this is why I believe that the appearance of a fairy or fairies in a dream, betokens something of significance. In one, charming dream that I experienced several years ago, I was seated inside and looked out the window to where snow lay on the ground. As I explain in my chapter **Dreams of Nature**, snow is my archetype of unrealised ambitions.

In the dream, I turned my attention to the pages of the book that I was reading. To my delight, a group of pink and mauve, sparkly fairies came to life on the page. It did not last for long, a few seconds maybe, but I woke up feeling warm and happy, and filled with the expectation of personal and professional advancement. And at a time when I was right down on my fortune, my expectations were fulfilled and my life changed. Be aware that bad fairies exist as well as good ones – remember what happened to the Sleeping Beauty?

CHOO-CHOOING IN YOUR DREAMS

Perhaps no dream symbol is more potent than that of the train, a meme of industrial strength that symbolised the steam age, the "iron horse" being the original wheeled vehicle that did not require a four-footed beast to propel it along. For nearly two hundred years, this meme has fed into our consciousness and the image of the train has become one of the most common dream tropes. The train serves as a paradigm for so many situations, but particularly that of the group of mainly unconnected people travelling to a common destination but with different purposes - Alfred Hitchcock knew what he was doing when he made his movie, *Strangers on a Train*. The dream train can be in a recognised station or in the middle of nowhere, stationary or moving purposefully across the landscape. The implications are obvious: are you making progress in your life or getting nowhere fast? Be aware of the landscape and its significant symbols: is it lush and green or barren and blasted? Are you chugging through town or countryside? Is the ground cultivated and agricultural or is it a tangled wilderness? Is it populated or deserted, filled with mountains and lakes, forests and rivers? As ever, context is everything.

Unlike in a car, someone else usually drives the train – but if you *are* in charge of the engine and feeling confident, then it may be time to embark upon a new venture. If you are a passenger, who are your travelling companions and what is their significance in your life? If strangers, are they friendly or threatening, young or old? If you find yourself agreeing too readily to do a fellow passenger's bidding, remember that Hitchcock movie?

VOYAGING ON YOUR DREAM BUS

Not long ago, I went through a phase when I had an entire series of dreams concerning travelling by bus. This is hardly surprising because I do get around that way quite often. In this case, it is a matter of pragmatism: a motorist will naturally dream of being on the highway, while sailors are bound to dream of the high seas. Always, the detail contains the meaning of a dream of this type. In one dream, I am trying to "get home" but keep missing the bus. In that hazy way of dreams, I realise that I am on the wrong side of the road. Another bus comes; I run and run – and catch it. To me, the meaning of this dream is pretty transparent. I am not actually trying to *get home* but get to a place of significance in my life. In this instance, it is to do with work, but for another person, it could be trying to start a relationship or family; whatever. The message is that if something you try on a daily basis is not drawing the desired results when it pops up in your dreams, then consider changing tack.

In another dream, I am with my sister and we are waiting for a bus. Oddly, we are at a terminus with many buses leaving before we attempt to board one. When we try, my sister succeeds but my feet get stuck and my footwear – old pair of slippers – falls off. But I persevere – and succeed in getting on the bus. It is apparent that in order to succeed at an endeavour, you sometimes have to shrug off old attitudes. My sister is an interesting diversion, but in the dream she represents another facet of my personality, the one that sets example and shows the way to succeed by switching ideas from old to new.

THE PLANE TRUTH

Planes are vehicles of modernism and aspiration. For years, I experienced a recurring dream in which I was dashing about, trying to get to an airport in which to catch a plane – but I would never get there. I would board the wrong train or taxi, or board a vehicle that stopped short of arriving at the airport or simply miss my lift, altogether. Eventually, I did board my plane, and it was glorious, soaring past other aircraft into which "we" could see, the sky grey and yellow – a dream as much about the colours involved, as the plane.

Questions to ask are: whether the journey takes place during the day or at night, what status do you occupy in the cabin, are other passengers present, do the stewards offer you anything, is the flight calm or turbulent, do you arrive in time or at all – or are you voyaging to an unknown destination? And once again, how are you feeling – happy, scared or excited?

People and relationships

MALE AND FEMALE

Everyone has both masculine and feminine traits in their personality. The person with the well-balanced personality manages to keep both traits in check and in harmony. In reality, debate rages around the definition of male and female qualities, and over which ones are "superior" to the others. Generally, male qualities are accepted as being *objective, rational, logical, focused, serious, analytic* and *decisive*. Qualities like *playfulness, creativity, subjectivity, dreaminess, paradoxical, emotional expression* and *empathy* are seen as female.

Whether one set of these qualities is "superior" to the other is just a point of view, though they do stand in opposition to one another, e.g., playful and serious. The fact is that the qualities of both sets are available to us, and both genders can make use of them. Just as contentious is whether a quality can be attributed to one gender or another. Although creativity falls into the female box, a great number of creative careers are followed by men, while many women excel in professions that involve logic and analytic thinking. Images of the opposite sex in dreams often work as a feedback system, indicating that you are depending too much on one personal quality.

I have already pointed out the caveat of Bruno Bettelheim, that the typical fairytale ending of the prince marrying the princess is a metaphorical way of indicating that the happiest lives follow those people who learn to balance apparently contradictory personality traits. The finest of qualities needs to be held in check for it to be of use to its owner. Creative projects, such as filmmaking, need as much hard planning and logical thinking as good writing and acting skill, to get off the ground.

PERSONAL EXPERIENCE

In one dream, I saw a man seated at a typewriter while I was insisting on a career as a copywriter. His presence indicated that, in order to succeed, I needed to combine hardheaded marketing with logical planning as much as creative thinking. Another experience was a series of dreams involving my late brother, who died before he could realise his professional potential. Each time, I dreamed that he and I were walking together across a snowy landscape. Eventually, he would indicate that he wanted me to dig in a particular place. I always resented this because I regarded digging as "masculine" work. On analysis, I found that my brother was the archetype of the under-developed part of me, indicating that I needed to use the traits associated with masculinity more often to achieve success. Incidentally, snow is the archetype of frozen potential, waiting to spring into life. I don't have these dreams anymore and I kind of miss them. And to my late brother, I say "thank you".

DREAMS AND LOVE

I have never, ever been one of those people who dream (while asleep) of connecting romantically with a dark stranger and then going on to experience the waking equivalent; it does happen, apparently. I have dreamed of love, though, about actual friends, family and fluffy animals and simply of doing the things I love. The majority of these dreams are meaningless in the sense that they do not carry any great portent. We absorb the things, people and events that surround us, every day, and it would be extraordinary if the dreamtime did not play them back occasionally. If you do dream of a way-out romantic encounter, then I say "lucky you!" but does it actually portend anything?

Whatever the run of oneiric events, I caution against signing up hastily with the nearest dating agency and seeking a partner that resembles closely your dream lover. Before wandering into a doomed, romantic entanglement, take a closer look at the subject of your encounter and consider what the dream is actually telling you. How accurately you can do this depends on how well you have recorded the details. Is the person known to you? If not, try to remember his or her eye colour, facial features and clothing. Consider the surroundings and if there were other people present and who they actually were. Did anyone speak and what did they say?

Take especial note of subjects and objects whose archetypes you have already established. It could be, for example, that a wiser and older person is advising or even warning you against rushing headlong into an affair that is similar, even superficially, to the one you have just broken off. Of course, it could be that the wise subject is encouraging you to take the plunge with a new love. Or the dream may not be about romance at all but the *love of your life*, a job, place or business. The dream may be a warning not to abandon a cherished career just because it is not going too well – your subconscious might be telling you to stay around and give it another chance. At the end of the day, how well you interpret the archetypes and symbols in a dream depends on how much practice you put into it. The more accurately you record your dreams and the more time you expend in dream analysis, the greater is your likelihood of gaining insight in what your next move is going to be.

PERSONAL EXPERIENCE

I can recount a "love story" that did actually happen to me. In the month of February several years ago, I dreamed I was looking at a paragraph of text – all about love – on a computer screen. *I wish I'd written that*, I remember thinking. And I awoke with the words of the actual love jingle in my head. I wrote them down immediately and searched the Internet, believing I must have heard them some place before – and drew a blank. I have since sold the jingle to a company for airing on Valentine's Day. I wish I could say more, but....

MEETING THE PARENTS

Like the majority of people, my dreams abound with images of my parents and as with all dreamtime imagery, the connotations of encountering Mum and Dad are subjective and ambivalent. This is much more so with this most profound of all connections. And much meaning resides in the gender of the dreamer, and whether the dream parent is dead or lives still. If you dream frequently about either or both parents interacting in various situations, it is likely that they are appearing not as "themselves" but acting as archetypes, that is, facets of your own personality or attitudes in your life, attitudes that might be holding you back from success in work, finance, love, whatever is important. In this case, you need to exercise archetype analysis to uncover what these attitudes are.

Think about what the word "father" means, particularly to you. It could mean love and affection, a companion to play ball and go fishing with. It could encompass authority, discipline, competitiveness, masculinity, strength, power, repression, loss or loneliness. The word "mother" might mean, an addiction to love and affection, warmth and security, serenity, friendship, femininity, fear of loss of sexual attractiveness, interference in relationships, and so on. Do not forget to place the archetype or types into your personal index of meanings.

PERSONAL EXPERIENCE

I experienced an entire series of dreams in which my father appeared every time I was working upon a problem related to what I did at work. I deciphered his presence as meaning that I should exercise more *control and authority* (one of my paternal archetypes) in what I did. In summary, the dream was not about my father but a warning from my subconscious about where my shortcomings were. But how do you tell if the image is *not* an archetype, that the parent is appearing as himself or herself?

One way to pinpoint this is to recall how you felt in the dream; did you feel detached from your parent or did you feel a strong or overwhelming emotional connection? A feeling of great love and affection normally means that the parent stands for him or herself. I have had some wonderful dreams about old times, about driving into the country or sitting on the beach with both my parents, with everyone as when we were all young and everything in the world was right. Such dreams do not usually carry a "message", but are little, golden gifts from the subconscious, reminding us that life was once wonderful and can be so again. Following a dream like this, I normally awaken and say, "Sub, thank you very much".

VERY GRANDPARENTS

Because I only ever knew one grandparent, my dreams experience rather a dearth of grandsires, which is rather a pity. In dreams, older and old parents stand for the wisdom and collected knowledge that younger people, no matter how clever and well intentioned, can never have. However, I do sometimes cross paths with an old man, whom I discovered to be the archetype of *a high achiever, possessing material wealth* and other less tangible accomplishments, such as wisdom. As I describe in **Dream Counsellors**, I have cast my old man as Magnus, a fount of wisdom. But do be careful; the old man can also be *decrepit*, bereft of material goods, knowledge, wisdom – everything, in fact.

DREAM SIBLINGS

In dreams, the interpretation of the appearance of a brother and sister will depend upon your gender, and how you relate to the sibling in reality. I have already explained that the appearance my brother, who died young-ish, is a reminder that life is short, and to just get on with it – whatever "it" happens to be. My sister and I frequently go shopping together, go to work, travel, go on holiday with her children – and all in my dreams – because she lives a nation away. Because I have but the one sister, it took me a long time to learn that these dreams were not actually about her, but my subconscious reminding me to take care of an unfinished aspect of my own life.

In families, siblings are often assigned – either consciously or unconsciously – complementary roles, by their parents and each other. For instance, there is the clever one, the pretty one, the practical one, and so forth, a matter that will be more apparent to those of you with a plentiful supply of siblings. In dreams, the appearance or displeasure of a certain sibling could be an admonition or encouragement about developing a personal trait.

Finding yourself in a place of work, most typically in an office environment, is most often an indication from your subconscious to pay attention to an issue concerning a relationship. If the "boss" is getting at you, it might be time to be firm with a person who is trying to dominate you. If you are in charge and still feel threatened by a colleague, it is possibly time to question what or who is bothering you. Here, it might be helpful to try the Gestalt method of analysis, and question all of the subjects and objects that appear in the dream.

CHILDREN IN DREAMS

Whether or not we have children directly in our lives, we all dream about them sometimes. Children are frail, unformed little human beings onto whom we pin our hopes for the future, theirs and ours. They need constant nurturing, are vulnerable to life-changes and unfortunately, to evil people. No wonder then, that we invest so much emotion in what we call childhood. Paradoxically, children in dreams also stand for the past, embodying unrealised hopes and possibly, survival of traumatic events.

I had a very happy childhood and often in dreams, I am a child again, reliving a Christmas past, or a day at the beach, or a ballet class, whatever. Dreams like this have very little meaning, except to offer an opportunity to vicariously experience a time that is long gone. The downside is that I do wake up feeling rather sad. However, since the dream experiences of people who have had forgettable childhoods are bound to be different, I know that this sadness for times past is a price worth paying for all of those golden years.

The meaning of a dream involving other children will be slanted according to whether you know the child – or not. In one dream, a good friend of mine took me to task for gratuitous mall shopping, among other things, and then proceeded to feed her little girl. On analysis, the dream was a warning, telling me to be careful when spending money. Mastery of handling finances paves the way to mastery of more responsible activity, i.e., feeding a child. Because of this significance, I believe that assuring dreams about very young people are manifest of healthy relations with other aspects of our personalities. In another dream, I saw a group of sleeping children when I was on my way to a job interview. The dream was calling upon me to develop the hidden (sleeping) and undeveloped (young children) areas of my life to prepare for greater success (the job interview).

A long time ago, I dreamed that I was with the family of a grown-up young man who insisted on holding onto a large, stone snail that used to serve as a playground fitting. His mother stepped forward and chivvied *him*, saying that there was nothing special about the snail. I awoke, acutely uncomfortable about the kidult refusing to let go of a trope from his past. I consulted my chart of archetypes and discovered than an *unknown male* in dreams stands for *fossilised thinking*. The man's mum was actually another part of my personality, urging the fossilised part of me to let go of my youth.

However, I have experienced a few nighttime chivvy-ings from the juniors. In one dream, I am working in a children's home. My living quarters are clean and comfortable but the children's apartments are disordered and squalid. I awoke most unsettled, and went through my client order book until I found – but the remainder of the story is too personal to finish here. The dream was a warning that I had unfinished work, that is, disordered as the children's quarters. Be aware that a dream such as this could refer to personal issues as much as business matters.

Scary movies are so filled with haunted – and haunting – children, that it has ever been my disappointment that I never encounter glassy-eyed, badly-behaved and downright terrifying little 'uns during my sleeping hours. On the contrary, my dream children have always been good, well behaved and even, angelic. If you have nighttime encounters with scary children, do not despair but work harder on uncovering those aspects of your life and personality that may be out of synch.

ROYALTY AND CELEBRITIES

Apparently, dreams of royal persons and celebrities are among the most cherished of nighttime imagery. After all, we seek out news of our favourite people by day, trying to copy their style and lifestyles and even, following them on social media. In dreams, royalty and celebrity are symbols of what is *best in us*. Overall, it is fortunate to dream about a celebrity but be aware that seeing or even meeting Placido Domingo does not mean that you are going to be a great singer; you either have the talent to sing or you do not. But what your subconscious may be indicating is that, if you develop a fine quality that is within you, for example, leadership, you have it within your grasp the possibility of establishing a great career.

The exact meaning of your dream, of course, will depend on the other happenings and imagery. In one dream, I was at the Palace, where an award-giving service was taking place. Without waiting to be invited, I stepped in front of Her Majesty. She ignored me and gave a medal to another person. On analysis, the dream was warning me to await my turn, stating that it is not a good idea to turn up at a place to which I had not been invited, and to try to take an award that I had not earned. All the same, I awoke upset and disappointed at having being ignored by this illustrious person. I took it as a symptom of my condition at the time, that I was not doing well. I waited for matters to improve and happily, they did.

EVENTS AND OCCASIONS

Dreams about birth and birthdays, deaths and people going away can be grouped under the banner *milestone dreams*. These dreams do not necessarily mean someone is going to be born, die or go away. Dreams reveal your fears and hopes, your thoughts and feelings on various matters. It could be that a milestone dream or a series of them is your subconscious trying to tell you that a certain phase of your life is – or should be – coming to a close. These dreams may also be telling you that *now* is a good time to begin something new. For many months, I had dreams in which it was my birthday. The circumstances were always different, but the hook was ever the same. In the dream, it was my birthday, but I was unhappy because I did not have anything to celebrate. Eventually, I began my copywriting career; as I became more successful, the birthday dreams diminished.

A recurring dream of death could be an indication that it is time to put the "for sale" sign on a jaded relationship or a played-out career. It's not all bad; in the same way as a dream of birth or a birthday could herald an ending, a dream of death is often an indication that something new and important is about to begin. Over time, I noticed that the image of Christmas kept popping up in my dreams. Most remarkably, very few of them actually took place at Christmas-time. Indeed, I have had several of these dreams during sultry, summer heat waves. Gradually, I realised that Christmas, which has all kinds of meaning in our lives – personal, social and cultural – had to be a significant personal archetype. On analysis, I found that Christmas in my dreams stood for a plethora of *good things in life*, insulation against cold and other extremes of weather, in short, *abundance and happiness*. However, Christmas also represents a complexity, taking place as it does at the coldest, bleakest time of year. On deeper analysis, I found that my dreams of Christmas happened in volatile situations, situations that were liable to slip into either great fortune or disaster. For example, I had a dream in which Mum and I were staying in a hotel. I was worried about having not enough money to pay the bill. When we awoke, we found that Christmas had come, and that there was more than enough money for us to stay in our luxury apartment. And soon afterwards, in reality, I really did experience a period good fortune.

Cosmic Dreams

The cosmos is a word that refers to the wider universe, the sky and the stars and the sun, moon and planets. The cosmos is all around us and often, it is so visible that we do not take any notice of it, which makes it the perfect allegory for how we regard our dreams. In this chapter, I include the more intangible and ethereal phenomena, such as light and colour, which we encounter on a daily basis and that often infiltrate our dreams. The cosmos has ever been a heavenly place, the earliest site of study open to the ancients, well, they *had* to gaze at something before the invention of television and the advent of literature. It was from this stargazing that mythology and world calendars and the prophetic understanding that we call astrology, emerged.

ASTROLOGY AND DREAMS

Astrology, defined loosely as a method of reading character and telling the future by looking at the position of planets in relation to the constellations at the time of a subject's birth, was recognised as a science until as recently as the Renaissance. Ancient cultures all had their own systems of astrology, including the Chinese and the Indians and the Babylonians. Later on, Hellenistic culture influenced this system, dividing the twelve zodiac signs into four groups of three, corresponding to the four recognised elements: earth (Taurus, Virgo and Capricorn), air (Libra, Aquarius and Gemini), fire (Leo, Aries and Sagittarius) and water (Pisces, Cancer and Scorpio).

The ancients knew intuitively that certain personality types predominated in the populations and tied these types to the juxtaposition of the ascendant constellation at the time of the subject's birth. In our time, the practice of astrology has slowly deflated to a curiosity column in magazines and popular publications, a distraction, a light aside to the more important news. However, there are yet serious practitioners of the craft who claim that astrology is a valid tool for wading through the vicissitudes of life. Practitioners claim that, like every other tool, it only works when you know how to use it, and that very few people ever *do* learn how to work it.

Today, whether we have faith in fortune telling or not, we all recognize character types; fiery forthwith people in contrast to subjects who are withdrawn and retiring. No one kind of personality is "superior" to another; all personalities contribute to the rich tapestry of life. However, certain personality traits may be useful in particular situations and the symbols that we encounter in dreams could be a nudge from the subconscious, an indication that we may need to develop a particular trait more in order to lead a successful life. In my chapter, **Meditative Exercises,** I stressed the importance of building a team of "dream counsellors", imaginary advisors that you can call upon at will to help you through the conundrums in your life, to help with creative imagination, with earning money and building relationships, and more. Here, it may be helpful to visualise the members of your team as zodiac symbols with character traits corresponding to those associated with the sign.

For instance, your grounded counsellor on whom you call for advice on practical matters can be the wise woman associated with Virgo-ans, while an oracle from a water jar (Aquarius) will instruct you on how to be mutable and flexible – be as creative as you dare. The analysis of your dream will depend on other circumstances, of course, but be aware that that dream-time talking goat you have encountered may be a Capricorn friend in disguise, offering advice or even, requesting help.

SWEETNESS AND LIGHT

Light has many meanings and works on so many levels that it would be extraordinary if we did not dream about it, sometimes. Light is brilliant and dazzling, both materially and ethereally. We call a wise person "enlightened". Light stands for purity and innocence, for cleanliness and freedom from worry. A load that is easy to carry is called light. Beams of light have divine implications, a characteristic that the artists of old made much use of. When depicting saints and other heavenly subjects on medieval altarpieces, the craftsmen placed areas of gold leaf to create haloes, rays of light and angels' wings. When the faithful saw the illustrations coruscating in flickering candlelight, they believed that they were seeing a vision of heaven.

With all this weight of meaning, it is inevitable that light creeps into the dusky world of dreams. I have had many dreams involving light and one stands out in memory. I am wandering around an old house, guided by the muted colour glowing in each room. I am aware of much cultural activity, in the form of paintings and wall hangings, of small groups of people enacting dramas and playing subdued music. In one room, I see a map of the ocean lying on a table, sepia-tinted and illustrated with those little pictures of fish, mermaids and monsters so beloved of medieval engravers. A woman, whom I sense to be the owner of the house, comes inside and begins pointing to areas on the map. Since then, I have identified her as the *dark woman*, the obscure side of me that I explained in my chapter, **Dream Archetypes**. But even before I had established this archetype, I knew the dream to be a warning, that I was neglecting the cultural side of my life. My obscure self was trying to point me in an appropriate direction, and I took heed of the warning. Much colour was in the dream, and colours do have specific meanings in dreams.

THE CHAKRA AND COLOUR IN DREAMS

The subject of the chakra has always fascinated me, you know, those fields of primal energy that permeate the various sites of our bodies, which sages on the subject have ever expressed as colour. This is unsurprising since it is the varying levels of energy or wavelengths of visible light waves that manifest as the colours that we are able to see. I say *visible* because the human eye can only perceive the wavelengths of a very narrow bandwidth of the entire visible spectrum. On reading about chakras, it was remarkable to see how the colours of the subtle body and the significance of colour in dreams concurred with one another.

The root chakra, coloured red, occupies the area below the waist. Red stands for sexual energy and it is no surprise that our lower quarters are the fount of new life. Above this zone is the solar plexus chakra, named after the network of nerves that radiates from there to the rest of the body. This chakra is yellow and orange in colour and is connected with mental activity. My dream dictionary meanwhile, classifies yellow as a "mental tint". Above this and the colour green is the heart chakra, connected with healing and serenity. In dreams, green involves nature and abundance. The blue-coloured throat chakra rules communication and in dreams, blue is a harbinger of prosperity in business. The indigo or third-eye chakra rules the head and face, and above it sits the violet crown chakra, which rules the more subtle, intuitive senses.

THE COLOUR SPECTRUM

In accordance with the majority of people, I sometimes dream in the colours of the natural world and sometimes, I dream in black and white. This has rarely any psychological import; the multicoloured dreams tend to happen when our brains are slightly more alert. A patch of a single colour appearing in a black and white dream is more likely to be of significance. When you record your dreams routinely, you will see certain colours popping up again and again. You might, say, dream of white horses or pink elephants. The creatures of your dream imagery certainly will have significance but initially, I would identify the archetype of the particular colour.

Write the colour of your focus upon a sheet of paper. Assume a relaxed posture either sitting or lying down. Think about the colour that recurs in your dream and what it means to you. For instance, blue could be "cold", "far away", "sea", "sky" and so on – or it could have a personal significance, like the colour of a loved one's eyes.

Soon, you will have so many associations that you will feel compelled to write them down. Make use of cultural tropes but do not be too quick to seize upon green as "environmental" or red as "danger". Remember, analysis is personal, not political. Remember also that a colour can have multiple and even, contradictory meanings. For me, black is an archetype of warmth, comfort and intriguingly, hidden treasures. Conversely, it is also an archetype of wasted energy, obscurity and death. The meaning of the colour ultimately depends on its context within the dream.

PERSONAL EXPERIENCE

Once, I dreamed that I was in a store. Piled on the counter were a number of bright-red objects, yet I felt unable to buy anything. I had already identified red as standing for excitement, glamour and - delusions of grandeur. At the time, I was doing well work wise and longing for retail therapy, but the dream was warning me not to go shopping – yet. It was a message that I reluctantly took on board. Not long after, my run of fortune came to a temporary but lengthy halt. In hindsight, my prudence had paid off and when I eventually did get to the stores, I shopped with pleasure – and hard cash!

THE COLOUR PURPLE

Heracles, the Greek super hero, is credited with the discovery of the colour purple – or rather, his dog is. One day, while walking along the seashore of the land of Canaan, also known as Phoenicia, he discovered that the beast's nose and mouth were stained purple from nuzzling among snails and molluscs. Eventually, Heracles presented King Phoenix with a purple cloak and Phoenicia became the ancient centre of the purple dye industry. For many centuries, only monarchs and nobles could wear the colour but by the 1900s', the birth of the chemical dye industry brought most shades of purple within reach of the common man – and most likely, woman. And in 1856, the Victorians went 'mauve mad' when William Henry Perkin brought the world *aniline*, the first organic synthetic purple dye. And of course, colours like mauve, violet and magenta all sit underneath the purple banner.

Purple has always been associated with heightened passion and it is not for nothing that the more emotional passages in a novel are often described as 'purple'. Artists physically make purple by mixing red – the 'hot' colour we associate with passion – with blue, a cooler colour. The colours of the sea, blue, green and purple occur at the higher frequency end of the colour spectrum, just below ultra violet, a colour that is outside the rather narrow range of the human optic nerve.

In one dream, I am on a non-specific quest of self-discovery. At the same time, I am wearing a purple cloak, an indication that I ought to be more open to meditative techniques as part of a daily routine –which proved to be good advice, actually. In another dream, I am trying to board a bus, but my feet get stuck in a hollow and my footwear falls off. In a panic, I look down and see that the "fake" footwear has fallen away to reveal purple slippers. I then board the bus easily. Purple is also an archetype of wealth, and in one very curious dream, two other women and I are dressed from head to foot in purple. We dash through a wood and all the time, I am hoping to impress my sister. This is a good example of a displacement dream, where facets of the personality appear as different people. My "sister" is actually the more practical side of me, whereas the two women represent other qualities – purpose and energy. Together, we are trying to impress my sister, that is, my practical side, by commanding more money, which is represented by the purple clothing. Do look in your dream diary for dreams involving purple, mauve and violet – the findings will astound you.

DREAMS OF SILVER

I have never had a "silver" dream from which I did not wake up with an intense feeling of longing. Silver is the colour of the moon and the stars, of daydreams and yearning and wishes unfulfilled. It is not for nothing that early cinema was named the silver screen, a light illusion that evaporated almost as soon as it appeared. Unlike gold, which is an archetype of tangible wealth, silver is the colour of the faraway and far-reaching, that which must be attained by personal effort. In a dream, uncovering a silver object is a desire to achieve a goal.

In one dream, I am looking at a group of people in a dark lake who are swimming towards a silver boat. On analysis, the boat is the object of my desire, the people swimming are aspects of my own personality, and the dark lake is uncertainty. By identifying these objects, the meaning of the dream becomes obvious; keep swimming or working towards whatever goal you want, and this will rescue you from uncertainty.

MANY SHADES OF GREY

So much for silver, but what of its less-bright cousin, grey? This colour actually has quite a good meaning; grey being the colour of the brain and of mental activity. In one dream, I am in an airport café and order ice cream. But before I can eat it, the pink ice cream slides on to the grey floor. I want to move onto my next journey stage, but it is far too early to board the plane. On analysis, the airport stands for *energy and activity, for moving on*. The pink of the ice cream is *non-intellectual activity*, whereas the grey tile stands for my intellect – grey matter. The dream seemed to be telling me that I will move on to greater intellectual feats, but it is a little too soon to move, yet – so take time out to enjoy less intellectual activity. In the longer term, the dream proved to be spot on.

DREAMS OF GOLD

Who does not love the sight of heaped gold coins, shining with the promise of plenty, even in dreams? Or indeed, dreams involving sunflowers or other items in that warm and promising colour, yellow. Every so often, I go through a spate of "yellow" dreams, where I encounter a significant feature in that effulgent colour. I have sat in many rooms with yellow walls – in reality, absent from my home. I have unlocked yellow doors, stared at intense golden flowers and even, cleaned numerous yellow floors, over and over. I would like to think that such omens betoken riches but oddly, dream imagery of unqualified wealth do not augur well for the person who is limited in pocket. My dream dictionary informs me that dreaming of wealth is a promise of penury for some time to come - but it is *very* hopeful to dream of *earning* money, a certain sign that matters will improve – lesson in life there? Yellow, closely associated with gold, is an archetype of sunshine and warmth, along with optimism, enthusiasm and energy. However, every up has a down, and gold and yellow are also associated with honey, which rhymes with money. This brings the darker associations of yellow into play, with the expression "honey money".

A dream featuring the colour yellow could be warning you to be aware – or even beware – of where your wealth is coming from – remember Pip's convict benefactor in *Great Expectations*? On surveying my dreams, I find that most of my visions of yellow involve me performing a mundane task, like the dream I described in my chapter, **The World of Work,** of cleaning linoleum, over and over. To me, these dreams are reminders that maintaining a good client portfolio is essential for healthy earnings – and to not sleep on a job – just like home maintenance, which must be done again and again.

THE BLUE OF THE NIGHT

Blue has ever been the colour of hope, of aspiration. Knowing that whoop-whooping feeling as you gaze at the azure heavens on a hot, summer's day, it is no wonder that the glut of uber-optimistic self-help literature on our bookshelves has been assigned the label "blue skies". Yet, blue is also tinged with melancholy; what we call *the blues* is a longing for *what has never been* or *might never be*, a sense that has given rise to ballads like *Blue Moon* and *Beyond the Blue Horizon*. Physically, blue light waves are shorter and vibrate more quickly than the long, slow waves at the red/yellow end of the visible spectrum. Like its siblings purple and violet, blue is associated with higher consciousness, with the rich, the rare and unattainable. And all of these qualities come into play when analysing the presence of blue in dreams.

PERSONAL EXPERIENCE

In one dream, I am staring at blue letters and numbers appearing on a computer screen, tapped in by a person unseen. On analysis, I worked this out to be a reference to my ancient and unfulfilled career in writing computer code. The blue writing gradually turns orange, my colours of energy and optimism. I interpreted the message of the dream as an admonition to move forward with optimism, even in the most hopeless of situations. I did – and new opportunities emerged. And the person unseen? That was me, I am certain, the future as yet unformed and waiting to emerge, like a butterfly from a chrysalis. As in all dream situations, colours work in combination with the other imagery.

WHITE NIGHTS

White is the colour of winter, ironically when the days are shortest and darkest. White symbolises purity, peace and cleanliness, but there is nothing tame or timorous about the shade. White light, actually a combination of all colours in the rainbow, is brilliant and strong, evoking the might of the thunderstorm with its loud crashes and flashes. In my dreams, white is the archetype of *information* (since documents tend to be white), energy, enthusiasm and optimism. A few years ago, I experienced a particularly resonant series of dreams with white as a prominent feature. In the final dream, the voice telling me to "learn to communicate" was the missing link for success in my copywriting career, which began soon afterwards.

DREAM NUMBERS

Very few people out there have *never* dreamed of winning a big money prize, either in a lottery or through another means. And many of us have longed for our dreamtime visions to hand over the magic set of numbers to gain this glittering prize! Alas, all requests by me to my subconscious have drawn a blank; dreaming just does not work like that. But it is true that certain numbers seem to occur over and over again in my life, and that on certain numbered days, I seem to fare better in everything than upon other days. For this reason, I always wake up feeling slightly happier on these numbered days than upon other days. Irrational, but...and I do notice certain numbers popping up again and again in dreams.

THREE IS A MAGIC NUMBER

Three has ever been a magic number; the world is filled with it. We talk of morning, noon and night, of past, present and future, of faith, hope and charity. In Greek mythology, there are three Graces while Christians believe there are three persons in the one God. The motif of the three wishes appears again and again in fairy tales. One apparent explanation for this is that placing a limit upon available wishes serves as a reminder that opportunities often are in short supply, and also as a warning against rash thinking and action. In a fairy tale, the hero or heroine only comes into his or her kingdom after the stock of wishes has been used wisely, and three aspects of the mind – courage, honesty, creativity? - are working in harmony.

Bruno Bettelheim offers a profound explanation for our tripartite way of thinking, namely that the recurrence of the number three in fairy tales – three little pigs – represents the three aspects of the mind, id, ego and superego.[41] Broadly speaking, we have three stages in life, youth, adulthood and old age. And existentially, we all have a past, we live in the present, and look forward to the future. Out of curiosity, I ran a word search "three" through my dream files, and was astonished to find that I had dreamed of three sets of various items, people and so on, no fewer than *twenty-six* times in five years. If this does not sound very many, I tried the same search with other numbers under ten - and the average score was four.

In one dream I encountered three princesses. In another dream, I *was* one of three princesses. I have dreamed a number of times of three children and in one, very bizarre dream (though it made sense on analysis) I dreamed of a beautiful baby girl – who had three legs. But the most recurring theme was that of encountering three anonymous men, all in different situations. The archetype of unknown males in my dream is *rationality* (helpful) and *fossilized thinking* (not very helpful). Again, the interpretation of any dream is dependent on the juxtaposition of all present motifs, and I analysed these dreams accordingly. Overall, the dreams were telling me that while rationality is most often a good quality, too much of it can result in fossilized thinking. The presence of three is, as I explained above, a warning to use all opportunities fully and wisely, because they may not always be available.

---

41   Bettelheim, *The Uses of Enchantment*, p. 36.

ASTRAL BODIES

The ancients believed that the position of the planets at the time of birth laid down the physical and personality traits that affected the life of the subject. In addition to personal destiny, celestial phenomena were portent in political situations; for example, a comet streaking across the sky heralded the birth/death of a king or political leader. But the cosmos is a crowded place and something is always happening out there; I expect that an astronomer today could join forces with an historian and detect a celestial event that happened in conjunction with every political change that the world has ever witnessed. Because of this cosmic link to the personal and political, few of us get through life without dreaming occasionally of suns and moons, stars, comets and planets other than Earth.

As with all dreams, the meaning of your cosmic symbols depends upon how they or it works in conjunction with other dream imagery. Generally, the sun, moon and stars are signs of good fortune but as with the ancients, it is not great news to see a comet. A clear moon is a particularly good symbol to see, but a clouded moon could indicate trouble ahead. Seeing the sun and stars in a dream can herald abundance, but only if the subject is willing to put great effort into an endeavour and to travel far in order to acquire it.

Much meaning derives from your actual position in a cosmic dream; are you in the sky, flying of your own accord, or inside of a plane or rocket ship? Are you flying the vehicle of your own accord or being piloted? Are you on the ground, looking through a window or are you outside with a crowd of people? Throughout your dream analysis, do not neglect to ask these questions.

THE MOON AND I....

Although the moon is visible to all and sundry for a sizeable chunk of the month, whether waxing or waning, I have had curiously few dreams concerning this cosmic object. Yet, the moon permeates cultural consciousness: with hit songs like *Blue Moon*, *The Moon and I*, and *Bad Moon Shining*, it had infiltrated story and song long before men set foot on its surface and today, it is the only cosmic body that we have ever physically reached. In narratives, when writers want to indicate a sinister or magical happening, they often place events against a backdrop of moon. Just witness this gem from the Bard:

> "Great business must be wrought ere noon:
> Upon the corner of the moon
> There hangs a vaporous drop profound;
> I'll catch it ere it come to ground:
> And that distill'd by magic sleights
> Shall raise such artificial sprites
> As by the strength of their illusion
> Shall draw him on to his confusion:" (*Macbeth*, 3:6:23-30)

The "him" is, of course, the hapless Macbeth, determined to grind all of Scotland to his will. But no matter. Only once in my lexicon of dream capture did the moon come out from behind the clouds. Overall, the moon stands for the feminine in your life, darkness – in the sense of unknown – and mystery. A full moon is a grand lady, clad in silver, striding through the night in her finery. A clouded moon is a warning that events might not run as smoothly as you hope – and the more cloud, the more you have to be wary of; following a dream about our celestial satellite, be extra careful when making decisions about business or relationships.

ALIENS R US

Carl Jung experienced a period of ill health, during which he heard voices both while awake and in dreams. He recorded everything that he heard and felt and for the remainder of his life, he travelled and lectured, forming friendships with priests and shamans. He recognised that particular tropes were common to certain cultures and wondered why, in the west, many people described a ghost they might have encountered as a "grey lady"? The UFO phenomenon that erupted during the 1950s captured his attention and made him wonder about flying saucers and little green men. It all begs the question: why have aliens so infiltrated our consciousness?

Increasing awareness of the vastness of the universe since the time of Galileo Galilei (1564-1642) has led to the body of the literature that we now call science fiction, most notably stories involving travel to unknown lands and encounters with fabulous creatures. One, sparkling example is *Gulliver's Travels* by Jonathan Swift (1667-1745) and the books of HG Wells (1866-1946). And since the inception of the film industry, moviemakers have been spinning yarns about the cosmos and its denizens. Whatever the context, aliens have always occupied an ambivalent place in our consciousness. On the one hand, scientists insist that in our vast cosmos, life besides that on planet Earth, simply must exist – and many of us agree with them. Yet, a number of people insist upon lumping the possibility of alien life together with psychic phenomena, such as ghosts and fairies. How you see aliens in dreams will depend upon which mindset that you occupy. Whereas dream fairies, as I explain in **Journeys, Energy, Travel**, tend to metaphorize the powers latent inside of us, aliens stand for fabulous possibilities that exist elsewhere, usually at a distance. Invariably, aliens and other creatures have powers that the human race does not possess.

PERSONAL EXPERIENCE

Sadly, I seldom dream about fantastical worlds or their denizens and I can actually number the dreams I have had about "little green men" on the fingers of one hand. The majority of my dreams tend to happen in mundane, home surroundings and the dream of aliens I recorded a number of years ago was no different. I was watching television in an unfamiliar lounge, awaiting an important (and unknown) event in the company of a group of unknown men.

I and a number of unidentified people are seated in a circle and suddenly, an "inner circle" of green, humanoid aliens with red-rimmed eyes, appear. They bag the best seats and make everyone feel uncomfortable. Although we have the rights to be *in situ*, the aliens treated us like the intruders, poking our ribs in a horrible and unnerving fashion. One of the men, a kindly reporter, tells me that it is OK to leave the lounge. I get up to go, but an alien grabs my ribs once more....and I wake up.

For a long while afterwards, I felt quite unsettled. When I put my dream analysis into practice, I realised that the *green* men stood for *unreadiness* and *awkwardness*; the things that I believed were holding my career back. The reporter and the other human males were the better, stronger part of me, telling me that it was fine to move forward – and it was. Be aware that not all alien dreams are of bad portent and I hope to report a hopeful one, sometime. With our increasing incursions into the cosmos, both in number and in extent, it looks like the alien dream is here to stay.

Dreams and the Unexplainable

RATIONALITY AND THE WEST

In the uber-developed Western world, we are hog-tied to rationality, accepting and trying to make sense of everything that we perceive with our five senses. In ancient Greece, the philosopher Euclid laid down the mathematics that we have studied right down the centuries, until the present day. In the seventeenth century, Galileo and Sir Isaac Newton theorized and established astronomical principles that held fast until the twentieth century.

Newton perceived the universe as an enormous, clockwork mechanism in which time flowed in one direction. But by the early twentieth century, scientists like Albert Einstein had begun discovering that Newton's figures just did not add up, and so he formed his own theory of general relativity. Today, with their theories of multi-verses and parallel universes, the quantum scientists are in accord with Einstein, theorizing that time is not always linear. If you consider their theories together with the wave-particle theory, we know that states are not definite. It is possible that dreaming is our link with this non-linear world, and that developing our faculty for dream analysis will provide an access channel to sources of knowledge other than we perceive through the five senses.

BRINGING OUT YOUR INNER SHAMAN

From Native American and Aboriginal tribes, to the Inuit of Alaska and the Sami of Lapland, practically every ancient culture has its version of the shaman. The shaman believes that the experiences of what we call *the present* are simply memories of the past and a precognition of what will happen in the future. If you have a problem or if you sense trouble ahead, the shaman can help you take action to circumvent it. The role of the shaman varies from culture to culture but generally, he can heal illness and envision the future, evoke memories and interpret dreams.

The shaman believes that during a dream, your soul goes to the *dreamtime* where everything about your past, future and present is known. What you learn there can enable you to have a say in your own future. The parallels with getting in touch with your subconscious are fairly apparent here – no surprise then that Carl Jung famously formed friendships with shamans during his travels.

THE COLLECTIVE UNCONSCIOUS

Early in his life, Jung saw a luminous figure coming from his mother's room. The head was detached from the neck and floated in the air in front of the body. Interestingly, Emilie Jung had suffered depression and other problems of a psychological nature and had reported previous "spiritual" activity in her bedroom. But the response of the Jung family was to send her for treatment in a psychiatric hospital. However, this experience had a profound effect upon the young Carl.

While yet a boy, he created his own private world in which he believed that he communicated with a mannequin that he had carved out of wood. Years later, he learned about tribal practices like belief in the magic of totems, which mirrored his own actions, a step to his forming theories about the *collective unconscious*. He theorized that the *collective unconscious* is a common store of remembered experiences and "memories" of events yet to happen, which our subconscious occasionally reveals to us in the form of dream imagery, usually when we sleep but sometimes, when we are daydreaming.

The *collective unconscious* is a strange concept, and one that I would find difficult to believe in, if I did not occasionally experience the following phenomenon. What happens is, I experience a vivid dream shot through with an extraordinary event or series thereof that do not make any sense. Within a short time – usually about a week – the real world colludes to make sense of the dream event. In short, the dream comes "true". There is nothing unusual about this; I know other persons who experience it also. Psychologists and other rationalists explain such occurrences by stressing that our brains are wired to look for patterns, and our matching actual events with dream-time tropes is just our channelling of consciousness of events towards remembered nocturnal images. Furthermore, since – *they say* - we are all the time dreaming, it is unsurprising that our dreams and real events do occasionally touch base.

Certainly this does happen, but I have too often dreamed about events that connect with a real-life event before it happens, for the incidence to simply be coincidental, a matter that keeping a dream diary has affirmed. And I believe also that this type of dreaming and the sixth sense are interconnected.

DEVELOPING THE SIXTH SENSE

For years, I have had many inexplicably spooky little experiences; you know, you are just thinking of a good friend that you have not spoken with in months or even years, the phone rings and – guess who? Or you are with a good friend or close member of the family, and you open your mouth to say something on a subject that you have previously not explored, but the friend beats you to it and refers to – guess what? Or you open a book at random requiring certain information and on the first leaf you expose – guess what you see? Or you suddenly decide to cancel a shopping trip or other excursion without precedent, and on the time when you *should* have been on the trip, the heavens open and drench everyone on the ground.

Rational friends have tried to explain these incidences away, suggesting that I could have channelled the information unconsciously, that I have possibly overheard an unfavourable weather forecast, buried the memory and then expressed my channelled unease by not wanting to go on the trip or excursion. If you have had such experiences, it could be that you often think of this particular good friend and that your more recent thoughts just happened to coincide with that phone call. Or maybe the book was biased at that particular page? Or since you and your relatives and friends share the same interests and concerns, it is unsurprising when thought/speech coincidences happen? I take all this rationality on board; yes, these things *do* happen, but certain of the coincidences that I have experienced have been so uncanny, for example, opening a brand-new unbiased phone directory made up of hundreds of thin paper pages – and finding the exact address that I needed right in front of me, that I still quake in wonderment, years following the happen-stance. And these events still take place.

DREAMS AND HIGHER PERCEPTION

Perception is the identification and interpretation of sensory information with which we use to build a picture of the environment. This information is channelled via our five "ordinary" senses, eyes, ears, nose, mouth and sense of touch. As we grow and develop mentally, other faculties come into play, memory, expectation and emotion, and the more mechanistic faculties drive us less and less often. Two people looking at the same subject – a rainbow, for example – and who are asked to describe it, will most likely write very different interpretations. Yet, both descriptions will be "true". This subjectivity is what drives creativity and ultimately, humanity.

In ancient Greece, scholars squabbled over which of our experiences, like the perception of colour, were truly objective. Even statisticians faced with the same set of figures can interpret the implications differently. One of the functions of dream analysis is to use the information sent us by our subconscious to create a more thorough picture of whatever situation/dilemma/trap we happen to be in, thus giving us the opportunity to take action more effectively.

THE POWER OF THE DREAM DIARY

Even before I began to keep a dream diary, I knew that I was *not* dreaming similar dreams all of the time. The only way that I could prove it – to me, at least – I got right down to the nitty-gritty of recording *all* of my recollected dreams, all of the time. If anything, the practice has increased my endorsement of Jung's theory of the collective unconscious. For instance, how do you explain a first cousin turning up, without any bidding or forewarning, following a dream about him or her – and this a person whom you haven't seen in years? Is this flesh-and-blood subject just another psychological "pattern", then? I have had dream experiences so uncanny that to relate them all here would make me seem like an old-time soothsayer, which I am not. What I do believe is that the dreamtime state brings the subject to a level of consciousness that occasionally results in prophetic dreams. This consciousness is available to everyone and can even be experienced during waking hours.

DREAMS AND THE UNEXPLAINABLE

In my exploration of the supernatural, I keep on coming across instances of dreamers experiencing strange and invariably bad dreams about people unknown to them. These episodes usually happen when the dreaming subject has moved to a new address, and are most often accompanied by other, unsettling events in the unfamiliar surroundings. Later on, the subject discovers that his or her dreams are related to actual, truthful events connected with the unfamiliar environment. One of the most notable of these occurrences is the story of *Dear David*, relating to the experiences of American writer, Adam Ellis (see **Appendix B**). The story is too lengthy to tell in full here. But in a nutshell, almost immediately on moving into a new apartment, Ellis began to experience unsettling dreams about a young boy with a misshapen head. Soon, the same apparition began to appear on the security cameras that he had placed about the apartment, shocking and grotesque images of a deformed young child – rationalists, explain *that* away!

These instances unsettle me greatly; in my study of dreaming, I have always learned that dreams stem from the psyche of the dreamer. I have written many times and in many ways, that we can all accept the *occasional* bad dream if we know that it stems from an imbalance in our lives, and that taking control of the situation enables us to vanquish the night time demons.

How horrible then, to be haunted by the traumas and events of other, unconnected lives. Invariably, the dreaming subject is prone to daytime exhaustion, with the attendant diminution of quality of life and work, which is why I dub these energy-draining experiences *mind vampires*. Worse, since the dream events are not related to the subject, he cannot control them – or can he?

TAKING CONTROL

We all know – or have known – people who exhaust and depress us, who make us feel "less than" when they are about. Now and again, one of these people may just step into a nighttime dream. This has happened to me. Surprisingly, I have had logical and rational dream conversations with subjects with whom I would never consider such a level of contact, during waking hours. In the majority of instances, I have gotten along better with the undesirable subject, following that. People who experience dreamtime contact with subjects they do *not* know feel bound to investigate the causes of other, domestic disturbances. On finally discovering the trauma or event that has triggered the haunting, the dreams invariably disappear. But occasionally, taking action is not possible.

I believe that subjects living in psychically active surroundings are prone to unsettling dreams, for the reasons that I point out in my **Sleep Disorders and Nightmares** chapter. When the subject learns the story of his or her surroundings, it is natural for the human mind to seize upon the trauma and make it the reason for his or her dreams, pinning the identity of the people and events in it with his or her own nocturnal images. I may be totally wrong; maybe actual ghosts *can* enter our dreams? Whatever you believe about ghosts, dream disorders do make life untenable for a considerable minority of people, which is why I have devoted the next chapter to explaining a little about them.

Sleep Disorders and Nightmares

Years ago, I experienced what could be seen as a very scary dream. I had watched *Paranormal Activity* (Oren Peli, 2007), that movie in which a middle-class young couple are bothered by a spook as they sleep. I thought then – and still do – that the movie was not particularly scary. A few weeks after seeing it, I was lying in bed, acutely aware of a shadowy humanoid form standing and leaning over me. My first instinct was to panic but then, the unreality of the situation struck me.

'You are nothing but a bad dream,' I said aloud – and I woke up! The room was empty and I was unafraid. Years later, I was pleased to read that *the* way of dealing with recurring nightmares is to do exactly what I did during that one-off dream, to *not* run away from whatever oneiric phantasm is bothering you, but to engage with and face it, or to fight it, whatever it takes. Doing this will rob the images of their power and they will go away.

Of course, how you deal with nocturnal phantasms depends on how scary they are, how often they visit you, and whether you are able to identify and vanquish the source of unease. The majority of us who have the occasional bad dream need only try making the statement or something like it that I charted above. Because the dreaming state is almost always one between sleeping and waking, the very act of trying to speak is usually enough to shock the body fully awake, and thus vanquish the phantasm. However, if you experience recurring frightening dreams that no amount of personal confronting will vanquish, then you do have a case for seeking clinical help. The following types of nightmare are the most common.

THE PURSUIT DREAM

Fewer things are more terrifying than that dry-mouthed, gut-churning sensation that is dreamtime pursuit. You are in some place, usually dark, when the feeling that someone – or something – is following you and that intends you harm. Sometimes, you can see the subject and sometimes not; whatever, you know that you have just got to get away.

You try to run but for whatever reason, you are rooted to the spot with legs that just will not work. Or when you attempt to move, the ground turns all soft and wobbly, lacking the tension that would allow your feet to move freely and quickly. Or you *are* actually running but whatever is in pursuit is gaining upon you, however quickly you move. You will do anything, go anywhere, to get away from *it*. You will jump from a cliff or out of a five-storey window, just to escape whatever horror. Luckily, you are only in a dream. And that is what you have to tell yourself when you wake up – or even before you wake up - that it *is* only a dream.

For the majority of people, pursuit phantasmagorias are one-off events. For a smaller number of people, the pursuit dreams recur, often with the same sequence of events. If this is your experience, then explore your life a little. It could be that someone at work is bothering you. Or an unwelcome suitor is foisting their attentions upon you. Your dream may even be *about* the person that is causing you pain. If this is so, then practical intervention, no matter how unpleasant, is the likeliest manoeuvre to solve a problem like this. Try confronting the pursuing subject in your imagination before doing so in actuality. Whatever happens, do *not* mention to the pursuing subject that they are entering your dreams. You will likely come across as silly and hysterical – and give the subject an *oeuvre* for even more unwanted attention. I stress once more that dream analysis is a tool to help you in your waking hours, *not* an entertainment spectacle for anyone else. If your pursuit dreams have no apparent cause but continue to recur, then you may be one of the minority that require medical help. Fortunately, sleep disturbances respond well to treatment.

THE ENTRAPMENT DREAM

Finding yourself trapped in a dream is just as unpleasant an experience as *impasse* in waking reality. In the dream, you might be in a locked room or cellar or attic, with no key in sight. Or you could find yourself trying to make a journey without a vehicle or ticket to your destination. Or you may be in a wilderness with no one in sight, and with no clue as to what to do next. Whatever the circumstances, the subject of an entrapment dream tends to feel overwhelmed by the environment, and that it is imperative to act immediately or be forever lost. This feeling, in turn, exacerbates the claustrophobic sensation, resulting in even more intense panic. You feel as if you are never going to escape the locked room or whatever the situation is. Invariably, you wake up sweating and hypo-ventilating, but glad to be awake – and free.

THE SOLUTIONS

Dreams like these have an obvious parallel in reality. It could be that you are frustrated in your role at work. Or you may be in a relationship that you want to say bye-bye to, but you just cannot bring yourself to "let down" the opposite number. Or if you are contented with everything – rare creature! – your subconscious could be warning you that your life won't always run as smoothly as it is doing *now*, that it is wise to continue to pursue the opportunities that will give you options. The solutions to situations of entrapment are in the main, practical.

In a quiet spot, take time out and imagine yourself in your dream predicament and working your way out of it. For example, waving at a passer-by from a window of the locked room could be signalling you to talk to a senior colleague about the possibility of promotion at work. Gouging a hole in that locked door could be an encouragement to undergo further training in prep for a better job. Relationships are a little trickier to sort out, but picturing these very practical escape actions could be your subconscious telling you to be honest and direct with those people who are closest to you.

SLEEP PARALYSIS: THE SUFFOCATION DREAM

When watching cases of true-life hauntings on TV, I have noticed how frequently inmates of afflicted households experience truly terrifying episodes of sleep paralysis. I do not disbelieve in the supernatural, but I am convinced that many of these episodes are symptomatic, rather than a cause, of the state of mind of a subject who is unlucky – or lucky; some people actually like it – to live in a psychically active house. The subject tends to live in a state of high anxiety, thus he is more prone to episodes of sleep paralysis. A number of scientists have put all occasions of haunting, alien abduction, and so on, down to sleep paralysis.

In a typical episode of sleep paralysis, the subject awakens and finds him or herself unable to move or speak. The subject may also experience a sensation of suffocation and a strong feeling that someone else is in the room. A number of these people actually see their nocturnal companion, and this hallucination can be grotesque and terrifying. Curiously, the phenomenon has given rise to many creative works, from the incubus and succubus of folklore, to Henri Fuseli's painting, *The Nightmare*. The paralysis can last from between a few minutes to an hour or more. David Pawson, the Bible scholar, identifies an incident in the *Song of Songs*, as sleep paralysis.[42]   I quote from the Fourth Poem:

I sleep, but my heart is awake. I hear my love knocking.

The subject of the poem, a wealthy young woman who has fallen

---

42   David Pawson, Unlocking the Bible (London: William Collins, 2015), p. 374.

passionately in love with a young nobleman, but is unable to marry him, constantly dreams about him. In the poem, she finally does wake up and opens the door that she has heard him knocking against, but he is not there. Her emotional state, of course, can explain the subject matter of her dreams, but what I find most significant here is the phrase "I sleep, but my heart is awake."

Experts believe that a condition called muscular atonia or weakness, causes the condition of sleep paralysis. The mind of the subject half awakens, but the body is not yet in tandem. Because the mind is in the hypnopompic state, the still-dreaming stage of waking up, the sensation of body paralysis leads the mind of the dreaming subject to believe that he or she is the victim of assault, and creates a narrative to explain his or her condition. Sleep paralysis can also occur when the mind is in the falling asleep or hypnagogic state. Earlier, I explained how it is during the hypnagogic and hypnopompic states that the mind is most likely to produce creative imagery. Most people respond to therapy that involves relaxation techniques and by exercising mental control when a frightening episode occurs. Over time, the patient grows calmer, more relaxed and less likely to engender the kind of anxiety that causes him or her to hallucinate.

NIGHTMARES AND DEPRESSION

Other than the experience that I describe above, my bad dreams have been few and far between, stemming mainly from eminently identifiable fears; worries over work and finance, health and impending challenges. The majority suffer from dreams where the scary element is a metaphor, an archetype of an everyday fear or stress. Remove the cause, and the dreams vanish. However, bad dreams do have a part to play in our mental health. Currently, clinical psychologists are using patients' dream patterns to diagnose illnesses such as depression (see **Appendix B**). Apparently, 3.9% of the healthy population experience persistent nightmares during

REM sleep while 28.4% of people suffering from depression do so. The broader point is that clinicians do take dreaming patterns and subject matter into account when diagnosing and treating psychological disorders, though I suspect there is much more work required in this area, to disentangle cause and effect.

OTHER DREAM PROBLEMS

It's like this. Every morning for days or even weeks on end, you wake up and immediately scribble down your exciting, intriguing or even scary blockbuster dream. Just when you think the A-list phantasms are going to go on forever, you go through a period when all attempts to capture a dream end in failure. It's not that you don't have any dreams; it's just that in that drowsy interval between waking and reaching for the pad and pen, the dream images evaporate like mist in the sun. You *know* you have been dreaming; you rack your brains and try, try, try to bring back those elusive images and words, sounds and feelings, but fail to do so. These "evasion" periods could last for days or even weeks and to a committed dream-hunter, they are most frustrating. My advice is - do not despair. It could be that your subconscious is going through a "clear-out" phase, just as you occasionally do in your home. The subconscious works in mysterious ways and is quite likely sifting and sorting through accumulated material in advance of sending new information through to the conscious mind. But never be idle: use these fallow intervals to go through your dream diary, reading and rereading those images and events scribbled down in haste and grossly under analysed, perhaps because you were under social or work pressure. Very likely, you will identify a new archetype, or even find the answer to a conundrum that has been irking you for some time – maybe this is what your subconscious *wants* you to do? Whatever you do, just continue focusing on your dreams and believing that somewhere in the imagery that your subconscious sends to you lie the answers to your problems.

When you least expect it, the blockbuster dreams will return. Believe me, they will.

WHAT ABOUT THOSE INCOMPREHENSIBLE WACKY DREAMS?

With a little effort and plenty of practice, expertise at analysing dreams does happen along eventually. But what about those wacky phantasms that seem to make no sense whatever? In one dream, I wake up and I am lying in my legitimate bed in my legitimate bedroom, etc. The sun is shining through the curtains and filled with the joys of life, I jump onto the lovely, floral carpet...eh? In reality, my carpet is plain beige!

Friend, I stamped roundly and soundly upon that floor, in expectation of the carpet reverting to its norm, but it did not. I walked from the bedroom, across the landing and into the living room where the furniture that I had bought (in reality) weeks earlier, was still in place. In short, everything was normal, except for that dratted floral carpet covering the entire floor.

I am looking about in wonderment, wondering what to do about the phantom carpet when I suddenly sink to the floor and wake up - in reality. You can guess what I did next – and the relief of finding my beloved beige carpet in place is still palpable.

Just over a year later, I wake up, get out of bed and check the time on my convenient dial clock, 9:40. I go into the bathroom, turn on the tap and instead of the normal rush of clear water, out comes thick, yellow mud. By now, a bathroom pipe is spouting the same substance all over the floor. In summary, instead of lying in a warm and relaxing bath as a prelude to getting up, I am wrestling about in a horror of muck and sludge. Next, I turn to mush in the muck and wake up for real. Again, you can guess what my priority was in the wake of *that* dream? Spookily, the time was 9:40, the same as in the dream. Like, how does a sleeping subject *know*?

I can only conclude that our subconscious sends us this phantasmagoria for the sheer fun of fooling our conscious brains into believing that something horrible is happening, just like a fairground ride in a haunted house? And to experience a rush of gratitude afterwards, that all is in order?

If so, thank you for the entertainment.

CONCLUSION

Wacky dreams encapsulate the fun part of dreaming, of course. But ultimately, our subconscious sends us this imagery for the better understanding of our environment and for personal empowerment. Repeating what I have written in the earlier part of this book about the fusion between the classical and the romantic, the subconscious can only indicate what tools that you have to make use of, in order to forge a better life. Ultimately, only your conscious, wide-awake mind and body can do the work. Nothing in nature is capricious and we would not have these varied states of mind if we were not meant to make use of them. And this is by no means the end of this subject. Even following years of dream analysis and putting ideas into action, I feel that I have only scratched the surface of this absorbing subject. I look forward to writing the next, exciting chapters.

Appendix A

A UNIVERSAL TALE

Aladdin and his Magic Lamp has always been my favourite story. I remember reading the story haltingly aloud at the age of four or five, after which there was no stopping me. I read story after story, but always returned to this, my favourite. But young as I was, there were aspects of the story that puzzled me, such the sorcerer or uncle requiring Aladdin to descend to the cavern to fetch the magic lantern – why did he not just go and get it, himself? When I was a few years older, I discovered that Aladdin had been extracted from the *1001 Nights*, a collection of tales from the time of Caliph Harun al-Rashid (763-809 AD).

Between the eighth and tenth centuries, Arab culture dominated the Mediterranean countries and so the tales infiltrated the folklore of the West. In time, *Aladdin* and *Ali Baba and the Forty Thieves* stood alongside *Cinderella* and *Snow White* in stature and popularity, and still do, a tribute to their universality and power over the imagination. In his book, *The Uses of Enchantment: The Meaning and Importance of Fairy Tales*, Bruno Bettelheim explains how the various characters and situations in a fairy tale are actually the various components of the psyche, running parallel with Sigmund Freud's theories of the *id*, *ego* and *superego*. Bettelheim describes how the events in a fairy tale are allegories for the maturing psyche, in short, the stages involved in personal growth and growing up. From this point of view, I decided to explore the way these components work in the tale of *Aladdin*.

GETTING AWAY FROM THE PARENTS

Once, in ancient China, the widow of a tailor called Mustapha had a son named Aladdin. Instead of following his late father's trade, the young man preferred to hang about the streets with his friends; you could say he was the original dissolute teenager. Aladdin does have big dreams, however. He has caught a glimpse of the beautiful Princess Badroulbadour in a street procession and is determined to win her heart. One day, a stranger announcing himself as Mustapha's brother, arrives at Aladdin's home and offers to set the young man up in business. This is first stage of Aladdin's personal growth, that is, getting away from the parental home.

The uncle takes Aladdin to a wilderness and knocks a stone in the ground with his rod. The stone rolls away to reveal steps leading to an underground cavern. The uncle tells Aladdin to descend the steps, find the lantern at the heart of the cavern and to bring it to him. He warns the young man not to let his robes touch the walls of the cavern or to dawdle on the mission. He gives Aladdin a ring to protect him. On the way down, Aladdin is enchanted with the riches that surround him, and he stuffs his pockets with jewels. When he finally finds the lamp, the uncle calls for him to hurry and bring it to him.

UNCONSCIOUS AND SUPERCONSCIOUS

Here, Aladdin is faced with a choice. He could simply ascend the steps and hand the lamp to his uncle, then return to the family home and squander the proceeds of the jewels he has gathered. However, Aladdin has the wit to know that if the lamp is so desirable for his uncle, then its powers must be available to him, Aladdin. This *burgeoning intelligence* is the second stage of his maturing mind. He refuses to ascend the steps, and the angry uncle replaces the stone and traps him underground. Here, Aladdin learns that personal growth does not come without pain or sacrifice.

Many writers have dismissed Aladdin's uncle as a greedy sorcerer who just wants to get his hands on the lamp, but I believe his place in the story is much more profound. A "real" sorcerer would have gotten the lamp and its power for himself, without the help of a naive adolescent, nor would he have given the youth a protective token. I believe that the uncle is Aladdin's dark twin, dark in the sense of unknown, the youth's *burgeoning consciousness*.

The uncle's guiding Aladdin to an underground place is actually an admonition for him to *dig deeper*, that is, to look into his *subconscious* for the knowledge and power he needs to survive and thrive in life. Aladdin's refusal to hand over the lamp is a rejection of superficiality in favour of real treasures. Alone in the dark, Aladdin inadvertently rubs the ring his uncle has given him. The genii of the ring appears and offers Aladdin one wish.

The youth asks (an appeal to the *superconscious*) to be taken back to his mother. He is promptly returned to the family home, where the delighted widow takes the lamp from her son. Preferring bright and shiny to old and grimy, the widow rubs the lamp and another, more powerful genii appears, offering Aladdin a second wish. He grants Aladdin all the wealth the youth needs to impress the Emperor and win the hand of the princess. He does this and succeeds, and Aladdin places his bride in a splendid palace. It has all seemed too easy and good to be true – and for Aladdin, it is.

THE MORIBUND MARRIAGE

Folktales often seem misogynistic, abounding with wicked stepmothers and stupid little girls who seem all too ready to kiss frogs and tell wolves where their grandmothers live. However, the role of gender in fairy tales is greatly misunderstood. More than in any other kind of fiction, folk tales require duality, that is, dichotomies of light and dark, good and evil, new and old. The gender split is often used to emphasise the differing strands in our personalities and the contradictions in our nature and behaviour.

In the second half of the story, Princess Badroulbadour displaces the widow (old and wise) as the less developed (young and inexperienced) component of Aladdin's nature. In her favouring of superficially bright and shiny over the old and genuine, she places the lamp in the hands of the disguised uncle (*Aladdin's subconscious*) and receives a worthless bauble in return. The uncle then uses the genii of the lamp to transport the princess and the palace to Mahgreb. Interestingly, the uncle does not harm the princess, which he could easily have done.

Both Aladdin and his princess have yet to learn to value each other. In his absence, she carelessly gives away the source of his power. Perhaps he has reverted to his former way of life, albeit in heightened social circumstances, carousing with his friends and neglecting his bride? Perhaps, like many husbands, he really does wish to consign the princess "to Mahgreb"? This failure on his part to treasure his marriage and his bride almost costs him his life. When the princess vanishes, the Emperor has Aladdin thrown into prison and condemned to death.

Aladdin now faces a third test. He can simply succumb to fate or take responsibility for his mistake. He chooses the latter path, the third stage in his growth. He summons the genii of the ring, who transports him to where his bride and uncle are. In the confrontation between nephew and uncle, (*conscious* and *subconscious*) Aladdin retrieves his lamp and bride - and defeats the uncle. Here, he is actually casting aside the adolescent part of himself; he has passed three tests and triumphed over his immaturity.

In the longer term, he becomes Emperor of his father-in-law's kingdom. In fighting with and defeating the darker facets of his personality, Aladdin has achieved maturity, personal happiness and autonomy.

Appendix B

HELPFUL LINKS

https://en.wikipedia.org/wiki/Robert_Moss
https://tinyurl.com/y4tuvfj8 (Gestalt)
http://www.msn.com/en-gb/health/mindandbody/could-your-nightmares-be-a-sign-of-depression/ar-AAbnLiH
https://www.banyanmentalhealth.com/2019/11/27/depression-and-dreams-how-mental-health-affects-your-dreams/
https://www.bustle.com/p/what-is-dear-david-here-is-everything-writer-adam-ellis-has-tweeted-about-his-haunted-apartment-from-start-to-finish-7714979
https://www.dailymail.co.uk/news/article-1353157/Ariana-Bardhaj-4-killed-fathers-sat-nav-caused-car-accident.html
In 2011, a young girl aged four dies when her father's sat-nav wrongly instructed him to take a "right" turn, while in 2013, a 52-year-old man drowned when his wife drove their car into a swollen stream, again on the instructions of a sat-nav.

Nobel prize winners on circadian rhythms.
https://www.nobelprize.org/prizes/medicine/2017/press-release/
Miwa Sado
https://www.insider.com/karoshi-how-overwork-in-japan-killed-miwa-sado-and-hundreds-like-her-2017-10

The Dreamcatcher
https://en.wikipedia.org/wiki/Dreamcatcher

The Dream Glossary

The Glossary is a collection of several of the more common terms and names relevant to dreaming and dream analysis. I have used bold text for those words that you stumble across in books and in blogs, but are not quite certain of the meaning or are unaware of the association, like "NREM" and "Gestalt" and "Cayce".

Absurd, The: a literary mode that makes use of dream imagery to describe impossible situations. It is closely linked to **Surrealism.**

Analysis (Dreams): Many methods of dream analysis are in use, for example, the hypnosis techniques of Sigmund **Freud** and Edgar **Cayce**, the shamanic method of Carl **Jung**, the **Gestalt** technique, or simply by identifying archetypes and placing them in context.

Anthropomorphism: the psychological tendency to ascribe human qualities to inanimate objects, for example, the *arms* of the chair, the *legs* of the table, the *face* of the clock.

Archetypes: Dream archetypes are those images and characters that appear again and again in various dream situations, over a period of time – just think of the same characters appearing in many different plays and movies. When analysed, each archetype can be interpreted as a facet of your own personality.

Aristotle believed that disturbance during sleep, for example, a draught or a faint noise, could trigger off a dream without waking up the subject. Free of the judgement of conscious hours, the sleeper accepts uncritically all of his fantastical experiences, and waking up brings that familiar jolt of surprise. Aristotle's theory is not a million miles removed from where our dream theory is now.

This was in contrast to his fellow Greeks, who were very superstitious. In addition to devotion to their gods, they believed in ghosts and portent through the Delphic and other temple oracles, and through dreamtime experiences. Plato's adherence to divination and belief in esoteric worlds reflected this, but his pupil rejected all notions of the supernatural and fortune telling in relation to dreaming.

Breton: Andre (1896-1966): French poet and founder of Surrealism, a mode in poetry and the visual arts, in which the imagination is freed of conventional constraints. Subsequently, Breton laid down connections with Giorgio de Chirico, Pablo Picasso and Max Ernst.

Carroll, Lewis: the pen-name of Charles Lutwidge Dodgson (1832-1898), an Oxford mathematician whose children's books *Alice in Wonderland* and *Alice Through The Looking Glass* are pivotal works in the development of the literary genre involving word play and bizarre imagery.

Cayce, Edgar: Cayce was a pioneer of dream analysis who developed his career as a hypnotist and healer following illness of his own. His method was to go into a trance and find an answer for the patient's problem. Because of this, Cayce was able to heal patients through correspondence rather than direct personal contact. Later on, he began lecturing on philosophy and experimenting with therapies like exposure to ultraviolet light, massage and diet, and healing with the help of gemstones. Today, many of these therapies are valid, with light therapy on offer to patients suffering from seasonal adjustment disorder or SAD. He believed that tapping the unconscious mind was a more certain channel to self-knowledge than the conscious, logical mind.

Collective unconscious: Carl Jung believed that our unconscious minds

190 ‽ MARY PHELAN

have access to a common store of remembered experiences and "memories" of events yet to happen, which our subconscious occasionally reveals to us in the form of dream imagery, usually when we sleep but sometimes, when we are daydreaming.

Consciousness: is the objective state of being awake and aware of what is happening in the environment, the flipside of being **unconscious**. However, researchers have identified varying **levels of awareness** within waking consciousness.

Daydreaming: Psychologists have written much on the nature of this subject. The majority of them agree that while daydreaming, the subject is in a state between waking and sleeping. One difference between the dreams of day and those of the night is that the conscious subject is in control of the imagery he or she perceives, is able to drive it and is in possession of potential for great creativity. Yet, the daydreaming state puts the subject in touch with his or her subconscious. Detached from the automotive mode of consciousness, it is the ideal place for thoughts to flow. Even when a daydream does not result in a great and wonderful idea – most often, it does not – experts agree (and daydreaming subjects affirm) that a short period of detachment from the *fully* conscious state is akin to taking a quick nap. The subject returns to consciousness once more, capable of tackling whatever task is in hand.

Dream: a dream is an image or series of images that rise – apparently uninvited - to the surface of our consciousness, usually shortly before awakening. The dream is a distillation of memories and experiences, fears and hopes, concatenated into a coded cocktail of images that appear to us in our sleep.

Dream capture: the process of recording dreams upon awakening, usually via text and voice recordings.

Dreamcatcher: a Native American object, usually a construction of wire, twigs and feathers, supposedly having the ability to "catch" the bad dreams of the sleeper.

Ducasse, Isidore-Lucien (1846-1870): the Comte de Lautreamont, his poetic work, *Les Chants De Maldoror,* contains the aphorism that underpins the creative mode known as **Surrealism**. In Canto VI, Ducasse described a young boy as: "beautiful as the chance meeting on a dissecting-table of a sewing-machine and an umbrella", and became forever the notional founder of the Surrealist mode. Born in Uruguay, he went to school in France, and excelled in philosophy, arithmetic and art. Romantic literature inspired him to begin writing, and he became a friend of Victor Hugo. Ducasse died of a fever in 1879.

Ego: the ego is merely the facet of self that we reveal to others, and its healthy functioning depends upon communication between the conscious and the unconscious. The better the communication, the healthier is the person and personality.

Freud, Sigmund: It was the lateral thinking of psychoanalyst Sigmund Freud that opened the way for the therapeutic interpretation of dreams. Freud's therapy involved hypnotising a patient until he or she could talk openly about everything, including intimate matters that were taboo in repressive, late nineteenth-century Vienna. He reasoned that if the intimate musings of a patient were symptomatic of his or her state of mind, the same must apply to the dream imagery that stems from the patient's unconscious. This pathology is equivalent to blood analysis for detecting physical disease. It was this engagement with the random juxtaposition of everyday objects – the crux of dreaming – that gave rise to the creative movement called **surrealism.**

Fuseli, Henri (1741-1826): a Swiss artist whose painting, *The Nightmare,* of a young woman lying asleep surrounded by grotesque creatures and a phantom horse, has become a seminal work in the lexicon of dream imagery.

Gestalt: During the 1890's, the Berlin School of Experimental Psychology became the centre for the practice of Gestalt or Gestaltism, its chief advocate being psychologist Kurt Koffka. His quotation: "the whole is other than the sum of its parts" has gone into history. Put simply, our conscious brains have a tendency to "compensate" for what we think is missing from a series of images or sounds.

Graphic designers and advertising executives use this phenomenon to great effect, nudging our brains into recognising brand names and associating consumables with our favourite sounds from the hit parade. In the real world, constant mental compensation can lead to a deficit of "true" knowledge, misperception and ultimately misunderstanding. Gestalt therapists bring their patients through various exercises, helping them see the total picture of a situation or even their own personalities, the raison d'etre of **dream analysis**.

Goya, Francisco de *(1746-1828)*: artist to two Spanish kings, Goya also worked anonymously, producing the Caprichos, a set of dream-like, satirical cartoons that warned the establishment on looking to the past, rather than engaging in the social progress that was taking place throughout Europe. *Imagination abandoned by Reason produces Monsters; united with her, she is the mother of the arts* is among his most famous pronouncements.

Hypnosis *you are now in a deep sleep,* says the hypnotherapist to his patient, in many a television thriller. What he actually does is put the patient into a stage between the waking and sleeping state, thus making him or her susceptible to suggestions like "you are now filled with confidence" or "you will find smoking a cigarette horrible". The theory is that the suggestion sinks into the subconscious of the patient and that he carries the effects of the session into everyday life. The word "hypnos" is Greek in origin, derived from Hypnus, the mythological personification of sleep, with Sonmnus being the Roman equivalent. This etymology has given rise to interesting word variants. When you are falling asleep, your brain is in a hypnogogic state and when you are emerging from dreaming sleep into wakefulness, your brain is in a hypnopompic state. In the hypnogogic state, your brain is highly open to suggestion, which is the basis of hypnosis.

Incubus: a male demon supposed to descend upon sleeping women and causing nightmares.

Individuation: This is a process whereby we develop powers and personality traits that our conscious mind has hitherto ignored or rejected, traits that our subconscious mind often reveals to us in dreams. Carl Jung developed this process for the better functioning of the self, redefining psychoanalysis as not just a treatment for the mentally ill, but an exercise whereby "normal" people discover new routes to living fuller and more rewarding lives.

Jung, Carl: Early in his life, Carl Jung saw a luminous figure coming from his mother's room. The head was detached from the neck and floated in the air in front of the body. The response of the Jung family was to send her for treatment in a psychiatric hospital but this experience had a profound effect upon Carl. While yet a boy, he created his own private world in which he believed that he communicated with a mannequin carved out of wood.

Years later, he learned about tribal practices like belief in totems, that mirrored his own actions, a step to his forming theories about the collective unconscious. Jung entered the University of Basel in 1895 to study medicine. His colleague, Eugen Bleuler, whom he met in the Burgholzi psychiatric hospital in Zurich, introduced him to Sigmund **Freud**. Initially, the two psychologists were in friendly, professional collaboration, but their theories began to diverge. Jung believed that dream images stemmed from the collective unconscious, a pool of ideas and visions that were possibly ancestral memories – hearkening back to the supernatural experience he shared with his mother. Freud stayed with the notion that all dream imagery stemmed from the repressed desires of the dreamer. In 1912, Jung published his book, *The Psychology of the Unconscious*, which led to his final break-up with Freud.

He recorded everything he heard and felt in his red notebook. For the remainder of his life, he travelled and lectured, forming friendships with priests and **shamans**. He recognised that particular tropes were common to certain cultures and wondered why, in the west, many people described a ghost they might have seen a "grey lady"? The UFO phenomenon that erupted during the 1950s captured his attention and made him wonder about "flying saucers" and "little green men". Jung also wrote much about **individuation**, that is, healing the person by balancing the personality with underdeveloped traits.

Kekule, Friedrich: The creative world is awash with tales of artists who dreamed and turned their downtime phantasms into daytime reality. Paul McCartney reputedly dreamed the lyrics of the hit song, *Yesterday*. Elias Howe found the solution to perfecting his invention, the sewing machine, when he dreamed of a fierce, spear-throwing tribe – and the spears all had holes close to the arrowheads.

The world of chemistry still charts how Friedrich Kekule's dream of an *ouroboros*, the ancient symbol of a snake swallowing its tail, enabled him to establish the structure of the benzene molecule. For years, he and other chemists had puzzled over it, and Kekule solved the mystery when he realised that it might be circular rather than linear. Interestingly, Kekule received this information in a daydream, a state of consciousness in between normal wakefulness and lucid awareness.

Levels of Awareness: Author Colin Wilson defined various levels of consciousness. State 1 is deep sleep or the non-rapid eye movement state or **NREM**. State 2 is both the **hypnagogic** (moving into sleep from wakefulness) and the **hypnopompic** (waking up after sleep), which are both rapid eye movement or **REM** states. State 3 is that groggy impaired awareness after just having woken up, but with dream imagery just vanished. State 4 is normal wakeful awareness and state 5 is lucid awareness, which Wilson defined as faculty X. This is a state of "superconsciousness", in which the subject experiences a kind of heightened reality, the kind of consciousness that inspires artists, writers and other creative people.

Researchers using electroencephalographs have established the objective existence of these states. Dream experts believe that everyone has the potential to reach all of them, even faculty X, since we experience "normal" awareness, and dreaming and dreamless sleep without even trying to.

Lilly, John C. (1915-2001): Born into a wealthy family, science held Lilly in fascination from his youth and he became a doctor following a spell in hospital. Later in life, his work in neurophysiology inspired novels and movies, such as Paddy Chayefsky's *Altered States*.

Lucid Awareness: see *Levels of Awareness*, above.

Lucid Dreams: a lucid dream is one in which the dreamer is aware that he or she is dreaming and tries, at least, to take an active role in the unfolding events.

Nightmares: 'You are nothing but a bad dream,' I said, on encountering a dark humanoid figure alongside my bed – and I woke up. The room was empty and I was unafraid. One accepted way of dealing with recurring nightmares is to not run away from whatever **oneiric** phantasm is bothering you, but to engage with and face it, to resist it, whatever strength of mind it takes. Doing this will rob the images of their power and they will go away.

The "defiance" method will work for the majority of us, since the very act of trying to speak is usually enough to shock the body fully awake, and thus vanquish the phantasm. However, if you are afflicted with frequent, frightening dreams that you cannot deal with, seek clinical help.

Night terrors: the majority of subjects that suffer from night terrors are young children. Seeing the subject sit up in bed with widened eyes as if in dread or terror of something, often with limbs trashing about, is the chief symptom. You cannot waken the subject, who usually falls asleep again. Later on, he or she has no recollection of the incident. Researchers have found that night terror victims are in the NREM or non-dreaming state of sleep. Children usually grow out of this affliction but adults who suffer night terrors require clinical attention, since the condition is closely related to **sleepwalking**.

Oneiric: the scientific term for dream-related experiences.

Ouspensky, Peter D. (1878-1947): born in what today is Ukraine, Ouspensky became a prolific writer and journalist on the subject of metaphysics. Notables such as Aldous Huxley and TS Elliot attended his lectures in London, and his publications include *Tertium Organum: The Third Canon of Thought, a Key to the Enigmas of the World.*

Prophetic dreams: numerous accounts exist of subjects experiencing dream imagery of events in advance of their occurrence. Many psychologists have dismissed the notion of prophecy in dreaming, theorizing that we are all dreaming all of the time about everything and that the events foretold by the seemingly prophetic dream would have happened anyway. There is no doubt a grain of truth in this; a stopped clock is right twice a day, they say. Keeping a dream diary is one way to discover if dreamtime brings on your prophetic powers, to establish if the **subconscious** mind has channels to knowledge that your normal, waking consciousness has not.

REM/NREM: During the 1950s, scientists used EEG equipment to establish the various wave frequencies given off by the mammalian brain throughout different states of consciousness, including sleep. Subsequent research in sleep clinics established that this REM or rapid-eye-movement phase of sleep is when the subject is most likely to experience bouts of vivid dreaming. Initially, we shut our eyes and fall into a deep sleep that lasts between 60 and 80 minutes, a phase known as NREM or nonsynchronized sleep. For the next 10 to 20 minutes, the brain stem gives off pulses of electrical activity. Presently, these pulses move until they finally shift to the occipital lobe, the area of the brain that controls the eyes. It is at this phase of sleep that the eyes of the subject begin to move rapidly underneath the lids. Incidentally, the REM phase is not a function of vision, since babies, foetuses and people without sight, experience it.

When the REM phase is over, the subject enters another 90-minute sleep cycle, that is, about 80 minutes of NREM sleep, followed by 10 or so minutes of REM. Clinical trials have established that on awakening, the majority of subjects are experiencing dreams during this time, with few dreams during the NREM phase. The healthy sleeper takes between six and eight hours sleep per night, and so experiences four to eight sleep cycles. As the night advances, the amount of NREM or deep sleep within a cycle decreases, with a correlated increase in the amount of REM or dreaming sleep. This explains why we experience our most vivid dreams towards morning.

Shaman: Every ancient culture has its version of the shaman, from Native American and Aboriginal tribes, to the Inuit of Alaska and the Sami of Lapland. The role of the shaman varies from culture to culture but generally, he can heal illness and envision the future, evoke memories and interpret dreams. If you have a problem or if you see trouble ahead, the shaman can help you take action to circumvent it. In the same way, shamanic interpretation of dreams can point you in the direction of opportunities. The shaman believes that during a dream, your soul goes to the *dreamtime* where everything about your past, future and present is known. What you learn there can enable you to have a say in your own future. The parallels with getting in touch with your subconscious are fairly apparent.

Shelley, Mary (1797-1851) : (nee Godwin) wife of Percy Bysshe Shelly, she authored *Frankenstein*, supposedly following a dream in which she saw a pair of eyes gazing at her from the chest of a human torso.

Sleepwalking: Many myths and theories exist around this condition, which is also known as somnambulism. Like night terrors, bouts of sleepwalking occur during the NREM stage of sleep, and the subject has no recollection of his or her activity when fully awakened. The difference is that the sleepwalker gets out of bed, moves around and in rarer cases, engages in daytime activity like getting dressed or even enacting a hobby. And like night terrors, the majority of afflicted subjects are children who usually grow out of it. But adults who are chronic sleepwalkers require clinical attention, since certain activities can place themselves and others, in danger.

Sleep paralysis: Experts believe that a condition called muscular atonia or weakness, causes sleep paralysis. This is a phenomenon that the majority of us experience, if we do at all, few episodes in our lifetimes. The subject awakens and finds him or herself unable to move or speak. He may also experience a sensation of suffocation and a strong feeling that someone else is in the room. A number of subjects actually see their nocturnal companion, and this hallucination can be grotesque and terrifying. The phenomenon has given rise to many creative works, from the incubus and succubus of folklore, to Henri Fuseli's painting, *The Nightmare*. The clinical explanation is that the mind of the subject half awakens but because of muscular atonia, the body is not yet in tandem. Because the mind is in the hypnopompic, the still-dreaming stage of waking up, the sensation of body paralysis leads him to believe that he or she is the victim of assault, and it creates a narrative to explain his or her condition. Sleep paralysis can also occur when the mind is in the falling asleep or hypnagogic state. Bouts can last from between a few minutes to an hour or more.

Generally, it is not a problem but for a minority, it is a serious condition that requires clinical help. Most people respond to therapy that involves relaxation techniques, and taking control when an episode occurs. Over time, the patient grows calmer, more relaxed and less likely to engender the kind of anxiety that causes him or her to hallucinate.

Stevenson, Robert Louis (1850-1894): prolific Scottish author of *Dr Jekyll and Mr Hyde*, the seminal work in which a respectable doctor who loses his sanity and his life when he discovers a drug that enables him to morph into two people. Stevenson, who was an invalid, reputedly wrote the novel following a drug-induced dream.

Subconscious: it is difficult to describe an entity that has no objective existence. But it may be helpful to liken the subconscious to a repository of dreams and memories that we keep in store, like placing objects in a cupboard for occasional use. Keeping them constantly in our conscious brain will only weigh us heavily and slow down our immediate mode of thinking. When we dream, we draw upon this repository of memories and impressions to construct the archetypes that act out our nocturnal dramas. Just as a total stranger can look into your closet and build a credible biography from the possessions that are important to you, continual scrutiny of your archetypes can reveal your state of mind – to you.

Succubus: a female demon supposed to descend upon sleeping men and causing nightmares.

Surrealism: In the wake of Andre Breton writing the *Surrealist Manifesto* in 1924, the surrealist artists and poets emerged, their dream imagery becoming part of popular culture, for example, the paintings of Salvador Dali, Giorgio de Chirico and Max Ernst. The artist Man Ray referred to a line in a poem "Les Chants de Maldoror": *beautiful as the chance meeting on a dissecting-table of a sewing-machine and an umbrella*. This word image provokes that queasy sensation as experienced in a dream when we encounter an unusual, unlikely or even unsettling juxtaposition of people and events, for example, seeing our best friend's mum in a compromising situation with a male relative of our own.

Unconscious: unlike the *subj*ective *sub*conscious, the *un*conscious state is an objective one, the NREM or deepest level of the sleeping brain in which the subject is responsive to neither sensation or dream imagery. Less common than we imagine, since most of our sleep time is spent in the REM state, experts believe that we need bouts of *un*consciousness for the body to become proactive in repairing bodily tissues and simply resting the brain in preparation for the rigours of the waking hours.

Walpole, Horace (1717-1797): son of Robert Walpole, he redesigned an old farm building in Strawberry Hill, Twickenham, transforming it into the Gothic themed house that it is today, It was there, reportedly following a dream about a falling helmet that he penned his seminal novel, *The Castle of Otranto*, in 1764 and ignited an insatiable readership for tales featuring maidens in peril, phantoms and crypts and bats in the belfries of rambling, ruined castles.

Wilson, Colin (1931-2013): English author and journalist whose work includes a range of science fiction and fantasy novels (The Space Vampires, The Mind Parasites), encyclopedias and biographies. In addition, he is author of studies on the supernatural and psychology.

Bibliography

Bettelheim, Bruno, *The Uses of Enchantment: The Meaning and Importance of Fairy Tales* (Penguin: London, 1991)

Bronte, Charlotte, *Jane Eyre*, ed. Margaret Smith (Oxford: Oxford University Press)

Burgess, Anthony, *English Literature* (Essex: Longman Group, 1974)

Cade, C Maxwell & Nona Coxhead, *The Awakened Mind: Biofeedback and the Development of Higher States of Awareness* (Dorset: Element Books, 1989)

Carroll, Lewis, *Alice's Adventures in Wonderland and Through the Looking-Glass*, ed. Roger Lancelyn Green (Oxford: Oxford's World Classics, 1982)

Edwards, Betty, *Drawing on the Right Side of the Brain: How to Unlock Your Hidden Artistic Talent* (London: Harper Collins, 1993)

Gilbert, Sandra M. and Susan Gubar, *The Madwoman in the Attic* (US: Yale University Press, 1984)

Gregory, Richard L, ed. *The Oxford Companion to the Mind* (Oxford: Oxford University Press, 1987)

MacKail, Davina, *The Dream Whisperer* (Hay House: London, 2010)

Mystic Dream Book (W. Foulsham & Co Ltd, London)

Ovid, *Metamorphoses*, Translated by David Raeburn (London: Penguin Classics, 2004)

Plato, *Republic*, translated by John Lewellen Davis and David James Vaughn, Stephen Watt (ed.) (London: Wordsworth Classics, 1997)

Radcliffe, Ann, ed. Chloe Chard, *The Romance of the Forest* (Oxford: Oxford University Press, 1986)

Shakespeare, William, *The Complete Works of William Shakespeare* (London: Collins, 1951)

Vaughn, William, *Romanticism and Art* (London: Thames and Hudson, 1978)

Williamson, JN (ed.), *How to Write Tales of Horror, Fantasy & Science Fiction* (London: Robinson Publishing, 1990)

Wright, David (ed), *English Romantic Verse* (London: Penguin Books, 1968)

Von Oech, Roger, *A Whack on the Side of the Head: How you can be More Creative* (Wellingborough: Thorsons Publishers Limited)

How to use the Table of Archetypes

I have included the **Table of Archetypes,** not to tell the reader what the symbols should mean to him, but to encourage him to begin building his own matrix of data. The material below is only a guide to what is possible, of course; I have excluded personal material about parents, friends and family, for obvious reasons but the reader will undoubtedly experience dream symbols such as these. The table is made of three columns, the symbol, the phenomenal and the sublime. The phenomenal centre column deals more with the concrete meaning of the symbol, while the sublime explores a little its metaphysical implications. Once more, I trust that compiling his own table will lend the reader many hours of fascination and empowerment.

Symbol	Phenomenal	Sublime
Airport	In the phenomenal world, an airport is a place where hellos and goodbyes are said. It is *a route of escape*.	The airport is the place where *my youngest dreams were centred upon*. It was not only a way to some other place, but *glamorous, exotic and aspirational* by itself.
Animals I like	Animals I like are fluffy, cuddly, friendly.	*They are predictable entities that know me.*
Animals I don't like	Animals I don't like are not cuddly or friendly.	*They are unpredictable entities that don't know me.*
Angels	In the phenomenal world, angels are a number of things, including business financiers and *compliant, willing humans*, often nurses.	In the sublime world, angels are pure spirit (created by god).
Art Galleries	An art gallery is filled with works and pictures (ideas). It can be grand and classical or else uber modern.	An art gallery is the archetype of the *dichotomy between access and exclusivity*.

Attaché Case	This is the archetype of *something that cannot be ignored.*	A case or bag is a vehicle for conveyance. *A bringer of news, good or bad,* it must never be ignored.
Baby	Babies are cute and cuddly, and filled with promise.	
Ballet	Ballet evokes white net and pink satin, tinkling piano music and mirrored walls, bodies moving in unison across bare boards – the *Apollonian.*	Ballet was my first, great desire. It evokes gilded opera houses in foreign cities, to fun and laughter at champagne-fuelled after-parties – the *Dionysian?*
Bath	The bath stands for cleanliness, comfort and joy, water and white enamel.	The bath also denotes vast expanses of water, i.e. the sea, drowning, *loss, sorrow* and *death, as denoted by the white enamel.*
Beach	The beach is a place, caught between sea and land, eternity and rock-solid certainty. The grains of sand are as old as time. They are also yellow (connection with money.)	The beach is made of sand, a material used in *construction.* Until used, however, it is a place of uncertainty, i.e., *shifting sands.* Archetype: *many good possibilities.*

Symbol	Phenomenal	Sublime
Bed	A bed provides *exquisite rest when you are happy* and feels like *a chamber of torture when you are not*. A bed can be dressed with linen that is *clean and fresh*, or *soiled and grubby*.	A bed is the archetype for the *cycles of life*; sex, birth, death, the *"chicken and egg"* conundrum. A bed stands for sleep (a rehearsal for death), *the end of everything* and dreams, the *beginning of everything*.
Bees	Bees in a dream is an archetype of *energy*, humming, buzziness and business, travelling, collecting honey	Bees are generally a good dream omen but come with a warning that there might be a *sting in the tail*.
Beige	Beige is the colour of tea, coffee, biscuits, chips – all desirable food. However, it is also the colour of mushrooms and of old ladies' clothes.	In the sublime world, *beige is a colour that the rich wear well*.
Birds	Birds stand for *travel, especially flight*. They *spread gossip by tweeting*. Sometimes, they have *beautiful plumage, especially birds of paradise*.	A dead duck *is an obsolete idea*. A dead bird is often *food*. The Birds is a movie by Alfred Hitchcock, *a warning about stranger danger*.

Black	Black is a symbol of warmth and comfort, richness and wonder, beauty, class, elegance, and objects of desire. Black stands for *hidden treasures*.	Black is a symbol of burnout, wasted energy, sleep, death, darkness and shade, obscurity and nonentity, shadows, cold and night.
Black and white, together	Black and white together often make a pretty pattern, for example, polka dots. However, the pattern could be a warning *not to be seduced by pretty appearances*.	Black and white together represent *dichotomies* in this life; good and bad, old and new, and so on. It also stands for *lack of movement*, rigidity, reactionism, conservatism.
Black and yellow, together	Black and yellow together, is the archetype of *awareness*, of *being on the alert*. It stands for busy, winged insects, like bees, for energy and productivity.	Black and yellow is also a warning of *possible hazards*.
Blood	Blood is evocative of pain and disease. It is a dark-red substance, sticky, smelly, muddy and dirty.	Blood is life-giving, the archetype of the *flow of population*.

Symbol	Phenomenal	Sublime
Blue	The colour blue is the archetype of *higher consciousness*. It evokes heaven, the sky, the sea and summertime. It stands for aspiration, as in *blue skies*.	Blue evokes lapis lazuli, high art, silk and velvet. It evokes *a melancholy longing* "the blues" for *what can never be*. It also stands for sex.
Boat	A boat is the archetype of a *hazardous journey*, of sea and rivers, water, wind, waves, storms, sinking, monsters. The journey can be of great beauty or terrible danger.	A boat is also a vessel that contains cargoes and people – possible link here with *monsters*.
Bridge	Bridges are pretty and come in many kinds; rustic, oriental, classical, grand, modern and basic.	A bridge is an archetype of *an entity that fills a gap*. It is a way towards something, and not necessarily permanent.
Camera	In the phenomenal world, a camera is an object of desire. It records images.	A camera enables the user to be a chronicler, social commentator and artist, all at once. A camera is the archetype of *frozen time, time standing still*.

Car	Cars are convenient, a symbol of fast-moving energy. It is a flash and trendy form of transport.	Cars are not desirable for me because *they are expensive and hazardous.*
Chemist and Pharmacist	Atoms, molecules, protons, neutrons, electrons, electromagnetism, forces of attraction. The chemist is also a driver and mechanic.	The chemist is *the archetype of the alchemist,* magus, magician, wiseman – what today we call the scientist. It is he who has the ability to zap his fingers and make things work. He is also the archetype of *forces of attraction and communication,* the winged Mercury, in fact.
Children	In the *phenomenal world,* children are very pretty. They are also noisy, messy consumers of time and energy. *In short, they are not desirable.*	In the sublime world, children are an *area of life that I have never explored.*
Chocolate	Chocolate is *unhealthy,* brown and sticky, filled with fat and sugar.	Chocolate is sweet to eat, creamy, dreamy, light and flowing, evoking harmony, like music. You could say it is the *music of the mouth.*

Symbol	Phenomenal	Sublime
Christmas	Christmas stands for *abundance*; food, clothing and other good things. It stands for family gatherings, for insulation against cold (circumstances) and for *happiness*.	Family gatherings can lead to quarrels. And gifts from other people are just as likely to be *things you don't want* (beware Greeks bearing gifts, etc).
Church	Phenomenally, it stands for architecture, history, past into present, beauty, peace, candles, coloured light, sensuality, sweet smells, hymns and chanting.	The church is *the archetype of compunction over choice*. It is a place where your outer self must manifest.
Cliff	A cliff is the archetype of the *edge of the world*; a place that you look up to or look down from.	Climbing a cliff is a dirty, dangerous heart-breaking job but *when you succeed, it is worth it*.
Clothes	In the material dimension, clothes are evocative of colour, fashion, extravagance.	Clothes are also known as garments, which are known as habits, which are hard to break, but are *what makes me who I am*.

Coloured Foil	In the phenomenal world, coloured foil stands for Christmas decorations, tinsel, stars, magic and transformation. However, its flipside is wrapped chocolates, gluttony and stagnation.	Coloured foil is the archetype of *the transformation of the ethereal into the material.*
Colours (many)	Many colours have implications of race, chemicals, opinions, emotions and interior design. They also represent Smarties, toys, Christmas and abundance.	Many colours could stand for one person having many opinions, or many people having the same opinion. Because of this, many colours in a dream together are the archetypes of *indecisiveness and undecidedness.*
Cord, cable and rope	A cord can tie, knot, tangle, strangle, rope off, choke off and kill. A cord is a communication line. An electric cable is another form of power. A cord that binds together represents strength.	A cord pulls things, expressing the power of other people over me and mine over other people. *A strand of rope represents a dichotomy, a struggle over being in control and out of control.*
Cow	Cows are special for me (I rarely eat meat). They represent warmth and gentleness.	They also stand for conservative resistance to change, all of the forces that stop me "moving on".

Symbol	Phenomenal	Sublime
Crowds	The crowd is a gathering of people who mourn or rejoice, revel or worship, mock or celebrate.	Above all, the *crowd conforms*.
Dance	Dancing; rhythm, tap, jazz, ballet, waltzing, jigging, reeling, whirling, twirling, stamping, spinning, hornpipe, folk, Morris – many types of dance.	Dance is the archetype of *something that I have always wanted to do/be*.
Death	Death is the archetype of facing the inevitable. Normally, it epitomises something that you do only once, but can also mean a new beginning.	In reality, we are scared of death, seeing it as a cold, lonely process, devoid of music and colour. The Grim Reaper personifies death, a pale-faced figure in a dark hood and carrying a scythe.
Documents	On a practical level, documents are made of paper and are usually white. They form the basis of receipts and invoices, bills, warnings and references. Also, they are made of trees.	At a metaphysical level, they are covered with words that can be trusted, but sometimes not. Documents "document" things; events that have happened. However, their meaning is ephemeral, subject to change; paper is soft, liable to collapse and crumple when squeezed.

Drugs	Drugs evoke blood, pain and needles. A drug can also induce a coma.	A drug is *the archetype of hyper*, awareness, activity and happiness.
Elephant	An elephant is a big, noisy and comical-looking animal. It has wrinkled skin, huge ears, trunk and tusks, and very big feet. It needs loads of space and food.	Elephants are highly intelligent, emotional and intuitive, yet are often made into figures of fun and even, abuse.
Gate	Gates are an annoyance, especially electronic ones. Such a gate reminds me of all of the horrors of being scrutinised and found wanting.	However, once I am through a gate, I feel better, like I have passed a test.
Fairies	Fairies are supernatural, mythological beings, *strongly associated with flowers.* They are deemed *capable of good works but also, great mischief.*	Often depicted as pretty, delicate and radiating light, fairies have inspired music, art and literature.
Female relatives and friends	Female friends are fun to be with, reminiscent of laughter and happiness.	In the sublime world, *female friends are the non-developed part of me*; sensible, logical, practical, sane, sociable, mentally balanced and down-to-earth.

Symbol	Phenomenal	Sublime
Fire	Fire is energy from the sun. It is warm and golden, a bringer of light and cooked food. It is evocative *of enlightenment, haloes and knowledge.* Fire can be destructive and dangerous, as in gunfire. It is *the same word used to get rid of someone from a job.*	In the sublime world, fire is emblematic of a three-pronged attack; romance, hope and despair. Fire stands for heat and light, orange and red, dancing, glancing energy – *romance.* Fire brings ruin and waste, devastation and destruction, leaving behind soot, cinders and ashes – *despair.* Fire stands for cleansing and rebirth, renewal and growth – *hope.*
Flood	The flood is of murky, grey and grubby water. It can also be dangerous.	The flood is *a rich, fertile soup of ideas.* It is also *a safety valve for highlighting weak spots.* The flood is despoiling but also cleansing. It can be the archetype of *abundance.*
Flowers	In the *phenomenal world,* flowers are brightly coloured, with lovely scents and shapes. They are possessed of almost preternatural beauty and make gardens the wonderful places that they are.	In my own personal world, flowers stand for *mourning, sadness and loss.* A *flowering* is the penultimate stage of the plant before it falls into decay.

Food (I like)	Food I like stands for all of the good things in life; colour, flavour, nutrition, society, money, *a way into things.*	
Food (I don't like)	Food I don't like causes me to feel fear, disgust, misery and conflict.	This is the archetype of all my fears coming to the surface, of *my life out of my control*
Forest	The phenomenal forest is a place of *growth and fertility*, birds, animals and trees.	The sublime forest is a place of secrets, lies and obscurity, of *getting lost and found.* It is a place of mystery and mythology, magic and enchantment.
Fridge	The fridge hums, buzzes, and uses power. It is a repository for food (the good things in life, words, ideas). It has a light inside, eg, enlightening. It is also high-maintenance, requiring constant cleaning, input and so forth.	The fridge is clean, cold and antiseptic, devoid of feeling. It stands upright; is alone, aloof, highly visible but paradoxically, "disconnected" from everything. It is a symbol of modernism, public yet disparate and indiscreet.

Symbol	Phenomenal	Sublime
Garden	In the phenomenal world, the garden *represents a number of dichotomies; hard labour and rest and repose, the fertility of grass and flowers and the sterility of stones and statues.* Overall, the garden is a place of privacy and beauty.	In the sublime world, the garden is a metaphor of unfolding time, the four seasons, *the universe.*
Ghosts	Ghosts are scary and mysterious. In fiction, they can be funny and friendly. . The very thought of a ghost is unsettling and disturbing. Personality wise, ghosts can be wilful and capricious.	Ghosts are immaterial, possibly the result of electromagnetic irregularity. Ghosts are transient and insubstantial – the possible archetype of impermanence.
Ginger	Ginger is a tangy, tasty, fiery, spicy, sweet, rich, syrupy, glowing colour, great on cats but not so good for humans. It makes great biscuits, soaps and stir-fries.	Ginger is the archetype of something that *is good for others but not so good for me.*

Glass	Glass can be both transparent and reflective; in short, it is always changing. Glass is brittle, beautiful and dangerous. When melted, glass is malleable.	Glass is the archetype of *reflection*, of seeing oneself (and others) more clearly, of deeper thought and evolution, modernism and revolution .
Green (colour anywhere, especially grass)	Green stands for fertility, growth and development, and food that *is good, but that I might not want to eat.*	It stands for nature in general and spring in particular; newness, innocence, youth and freshness.
Grey	Grey is the archetype of *obfuscation, obscuration and uncertainty*, ie, a grey area. It is also the archetype *of much intellectual activity.*	Grey can be *quite beautiful*, as in silver grey, standing for *everything I want and want to be*. It is also the colour of *shadows, old age and mortality.*
Grid	In design, the grid evokes coffering, waffles and check shirts. The grid is versatile in that it can be monochrome or made in many colours.	The grid is the archetype of power, strength and networking, of order, geometry and completeness, of harmony and symmetry. It is a scheme or frame of reference.

Symbol	Phenomenal	Sublime
Hair	Hair is lovely, desirable stuff. It is symbolic of beauty, luxury and abundance. Abundant hair stands for growth.	Hair is *desirable currency*. Like money, *it is something that I never have enough of.* Hair is the *archetype of blossoming*; of careers, relationships, health and financial fortunes.
Holes	The sense capsules, like eye sockets and so on, are holes of a kind, our link with the outside world. Holes also stand for weakness, hidden dangers and loss.	In dreams, *a series of holes is the archetype of the dynamic flow of thought*, of enlightenment and incredible energy, a channel from one world to another, e.g. black holes.
Holiday	A holiday is a means to get away from it all, to escape the ordinary, the everyday, the mundane. It can mean travelling to foreign cities, meeting new people or simply a period of rest, spent at home.	Whatever, a holiday is *a means to see the world through new eyes.*
Home	In the *phenomenal world*, the house & place I grew up in seemed warm and cosy I was happy there.	In the *sublime world*, the house/place I grew up in is a place I don't want to be but am always being pulled back towards. *It represents a stifling, a dearth of growth.*

Horse	Horses evoke breeding and beauty, speed and strength, intelligence and aspiration. The beasts evoke the Wild West, prairies and cowboys. Horses labour in both the town and the countryside.	The world of myth is filled with horses; the white chalk horses on English hillsides, Pegasus and Black Beauty, and fairy tale horses like Falada. The horse in Fuseli's "Nightmare" is scary.
Hospital	Aesthetically, hospitals are often ugly. Inside, they are brightly lit, uncomfortable and filled with people knowledgeable in many disciplines. In a way, they archetype *university*.	A hospital is a place where you do not want to go, but sometimes might need to. It is a *place of healing*, although being there means spending time alongside of the sick.
Houses (new) and buildings	Modern houses are bright and cheery, but the people who live inside of them do not often reflect this value.	In the sublime world, modernism stands for a conflict of values, conservative people in a new world.

Symbol	Phenomenal	Sublime
Houses (old and dilapidated)	In the *phenomenal* world, the dilapidated old house has parasites growing on and in its walls; wasps, spiders, birds and rodents. There is also moss, lichen and creepers. The house is liable to *haunting*.	In the *sublime* world, the old house is the *archetype of the past, of everything I want to get away from.*
Houses (old and grand)	It stands for heaven on earth, having many treasure-filled rooms, and standing for many lives lived in it.	A grand house also represents *a dichotomy*; one of *nefarious and dark deeds* in a fine setting.
Human Bones	Bones are mineral. They epitomise a framework; rigidity and strength. Paradoxically, they also symbolise the vapidity of ghosts and hauntings.	In the sublime world, *human bones are the link between wealth and death, i.e, legacies.* The French for skeleton is ombré, which also means "shadow".
Italy	Italy evokes great food, passion and intense feeling. It is redolent of sunshine and flowers, the avant garde in design and fashion, of futurism and of movement.	Italy is also redolent of old buildings and ancient ruins, of clericism and religion, of ancient secrets and the supernatural.

Journey (international)	This is the *archetype of new ideas*, movement and networking, energy, vibration and conveyance vehicles.	Conversely, this is the archetype of *malfunction* and *culture shock, obscure language, loneliness* and *loss of identity*.
Journey (local)	Local journeys are inconvenient, expensive and boring.	Local journeys are the archetypes of *things I may not want to do*.
Key	Keys are metallic and magnetic, attracting things and openings things. The key is *a way into something*.	The key is an adjunct to locks and chains, *ties and responsibilities*.
Kitchen	The kitchen can be messy with strange smells, a place where I seem to be forever cleaning.	The kitchen is a place I never excel & I don't always want to be. It can be centre of home, a refuge, a place of nourishment, where magic things happen.
Light	Light means *easy to carry*. It is brilliant, dazzling and coruscating. Light is candlelight on gold leaf, luminescence, phosphorescence and fluorescence. Light means nice and easy to eat, purity and innocence. Light is daylight, wavelength and colour.	Light is archetype of throwing light on a matter, which is why illustrations used be called illuminations. Light is inspiration and enlightenment. Light is celestial; the sun, moon and stars.

Symbol	Phenomenal	Sublime
Lilac	Lilac is made of short, high-frequency waves, sharp scent, pretty colour, cleanliness and purity.	Lilac is *the archetype of the limit of time.*
Maid	The (usually female) maid is seen as servile, clean and ordered. She often wears a black and white uniform. She is industrious and has a "can-do" attitude.	The maid is a warning to dreamers to not be too willing to do the bidding of other people.
Medical treatment	Medical treatment often has unpleasant side effects, but can be the only route to personal and professional progress.	Medical treatment is the archetype of uncertainty. When a person is uncertain in a new situation they can be anxious although there is also the possibility of metamorphosis.
Money	Money buys happiness, *freedom, great companions, glamour, elegance,* luxury, comfort and ease.	Money is the reason for greed and inequality, in short, *the reason the earth is being plundered.*

Mother	Physiologically, Mother heralds pregnancy, birth and breastfeeding. Psychologically, she is nurturing and caring.	*The mother is the archetype of the feminine.* She is the fount of all life, the cycle from birth to death.
Mould & Toadstools	Mould is nasty, smelly, ugly, undesirable, the result of anaerobic respiration, *a sign that something is out of order.*	It can be a useful indicator of malfunction, a warning.
Mountain	Mountains are big, beautiful and dangerous, often the source of mineral wealth.	The mountain is the archetype of an *obstacle*, one that prevents you doing what you want, like age or illness.
Mud	In the phenomenal world, mud is a rich, fertile soup from which trees and plants grow. It is *the fount of all life.* Many people don't like it because *it is smelly and obfuscating.*	In the sublime world, *mud stands for ideas.* However, it is all too easy to get *bogged down in and swamped by ideas* that are never put into action.

Symbol	Phenomenal	Sublime
Music	Materially, music is linked to orchestras, the Beatles, Rolling Stones and many other musicians.	Music is the archetype *of making order of disorder*. It is the bridge between thought (spirit) and matter. Music is linked to chaos theory, the universe and the cosmos.
Old Man	The old man can *be a high achiever, possessing material* wealth and other less tangible accomplishments, such as wisdom.	The old man is the archetype of extremes, *of opposite ends of the spectrum*.
Orange	Orange is the archetype of *endings and beginnings*, the colour of *sunrise and sunset*. It is the colour of sweetness and light, energy and fire, optimism, blossoms and weddings, fruit and nutrition.	Cultural meme: *the future is orange*.
Ornaments	An ornament can be made of glass, crystal, china, porcelain, silver, gold, brass, copper, pewter, spelter, wood or plaster.	*Ornaments represent a dichotomy*. They can be cheap, garish and ugly, to the point of drawing laughter. They can also be valuable, beautiful and cherished.
Pink	Pink stands for candy, sweetness, lost innocence, childhood and fun.	Pink is the archetype of *non-intellectual activity*.

Public buildings; churches, schools.	The archetype of any public building is a middle-aged woman. Her hair is grey and in a bun, and there are glasses perched on her nose.	Though her figure is "matronly", there is nothing warm and sweet about her manner, which is icy and forbidding. In short, *she forbids everything that you want to do.*
Purple	The colour purple works on four levels. Materially, it stands for Cadbury's chocolate, mussel shells and heliotrope flowers, the seashore and sunshine. Sensually, it is warmth and melting sweetness.	At a worldly level, it represents Tyrian purple, exclusivity, abundance, wealth and majesty. Mystically, it stands for heightened consciousness and higher thinking, *the archetype for things still out of reach.*
Red	Red is the colour of brains and brain power, energy, birth, blood, fast-moving events, heat, anger, danger, forbidden pleasures, sex, yummy food and a sign that *time that is running out.*	Red is a symbol for *delusions of grandeur,* royalty, roses, wine, red silk dresses and perfume, things that are *nice to have but you don't need.*
Restaurant	A restaurant is a place of people and a place of food, *denoting ambience.*	Ambience can also translate into *arrogance* and *entitlement.*

Symbol	Phenomenal	Sublime
River	Rivers are *cyclical*, birth, life, fertility, progression & death. Rivers are *material*, sustaining boats and people, fishing and swimming. Rivers are *mythical*, giving rise to folklore & legend.	A river is the archetype *of warning, not to get carried away.*
Road	A road is *a way through to something; everything.*	Roads are exposed, often dangerous.
Sea	The sea is linked to water. It stands for time, tide and eternity. Its colours, blue, green, purple, et al, occur at the "higher" end of the spectrum, eg. *higher consciousness.*	The sea is the archetype of the *subconscious*, a kind of Underworld, a repository of dreams and memories. When the sea is *calm, it mirrors the self*
School	A school is a place of learning, in which many disciplines are taught. A industrious person may reap great rewards through hard work.	At school, a person is subject to severe discipline and hard work. Whatever the rewards, it is a place of mild suffering or, at least, *not always a place to be happy.*

Shoes	A shoe embodies the idea of *fashion and style*.	Shoes represent a *conundrum*, that is, does the wearer control the shoes or vice versa? The shoe also embodies a dilemma, that is, to *go to an old, well-worn place* or find somewhere that is *new and exciting?*
Snow	Snow resembles icing sugar. It stands for sweetness, melting bliss, ethereality, *nirvana and obscurity* Snow is invasive & infiltrating, which can be good or not good.	Snow is icy cold, standing for obscurity and *death of dreams*. It stands for whiteness and modernity, an archetype of *unrealised dreams*.
Store	In the phenomenal world, a store is a repository for goods (ideas, thoughts, events, feelings?). A store is also a place where you can buy goods.	Subliminally, the store is a reminder that everything that you do/take/say must eventually *be paid for*. We use the word as a figure of speech, i.e, "what does the future hold in store?"
Sweets	In the phenomenal world, sweets are lovely to eat but bad for teeth, skin, hair, and ruinous to internal organs. *Sweets are tempting, irresistible and ruinous.*	In the *sublime world, sweets are glamorous*; red, pink and yellow, all the "bad" colours (honey money, delusions of grandeur and non-intellectual activity.

Symbol	Phenomenal	Sublime
Swimming Pool	In the phenomenal world, the pool is cool; calm when deserted and wavy and noisy when occupied. It is a place where ancient meets modern, an edifice of glass and marble, a place to achieve health, strength and beauty.	In the sublime world, the swimming pool is *a place where I want to be, doing what I like.*
Theatre	A theatre is a place where dramas are staged and human emotions run rampant.	A theatre is a repository of dreams, of love, beauty, happiness, colour, music, drama, pathos, pain, fear, anger, all that is ephemeral.
Three	Three is a magic number, as in Holy Trinity, beginning, middle and end, three wishes, three Graces, three bears, three little pigs; indeed, the tripartite is universal.	Three also has a dark side. Three is an *odd* number. Two is company, but three is a crowd.
Tickets	The material of a ticket, plastic, paper or whatever, is immaterial.	A ticket is the archetype of *that which must be paid for.* A ticket is a passport to someplace, a licence to do something special. Always, however, there is a price to pay.

Toys	Toys are *little things that ape reality*. A dream about toys could mean that important matters are moving beyond your control.	The sublime world is filled with instances of haunted toys, especially dolls, that are reputed to move of their own accord.
Tree	A tree represents the *strong, rooted* and lovely, attracting life and colour, supplying food and shelter.	The tree is an arcane symbol of life, linking heaven – sky – with earth.
Telephone	Though not highly visible, the telephone is a pervasive instrument, intrusive, invasive and publicly engaging. It is very high maintenance in terms of money	The telephone hums and buzzes with energy. It is a symbol of modernism and enlightenment, a *"work-enabler", a bringer of words, ideas, thoughts and conversation.*
Tunnel	In a tunnel, you cannot see what is going on overhead. There is a dearth of light and air, and often, smells.	A tunnel is the archetype of *a way into a world*; but *the least good of a number of options.*

Symbol	Phenomenal	Sublime
Wasps	Wasps are fierce, biting insects. Their danger is signified by their black and yellow colour, warning of vicious and poisonous stings. They fly into where you don't want them to be.	The only redemption of the wasp is the ability to fly. In the sublime world, the wasp signifies *news that you might not want to hear but sometimes, you need to hear.* The insect is the archetype of *rumour and gossip.*
Water	Dreams of water (rain, streams and sea) are usually fortunate. Stagnant water is not so favourable, however.	Water symbolises cleanliness, refreshment, recreation and fitness (swimming!), and loveliness.
White	White is the colour of paper envelopes that may contain money, information, good news or bad.	White is the colour of snow and cold, fridges, sterility, cleanliness and death, since *dead things are always white*
Winter	In the phenomenal world, Christmas means short, dark days, cold, snow, rain, wind, frost, ice and mud. It also means boredom.	Winter is the *archetype of longings.* It stands for Christmas gifts, loads of food and warmth, time with family.

Wolf	The wolf is a mass of contradictions.. He is hungry, hairy, friendly, furry, cuddly, fierce, ravenous, loyal, passionate, dedicated, focussed, intelligent.	The wolf is *the archetype of paradox*. He is the noble savage, living in mountains and forests, and the dedicated family animal, watching his family of cubs.
Yellow	Yellow stands for *gold and sunshine*, summer, warmth and happiness, also *healing*, honey and yellow flowers, egg yolk, and syrup. It has connotations of sweetness and cornfields, of summer days in the country, and golden beaches.	Although yellow is a "youthful" colour, it does not denote innocence. When combined with money (gold), honey has dubious connotations. .

Index

Trees 86, 113, 114, 115, 212, 215, 223

Tunnel 116, 229

U

UFO 31, 166, 194

Unconscious 28, 29, 30, 31, 39, 49, 51, 59, 64, 90, 91, 101, 169, 170, 172, 189, 190, 191, 193, 200

Underworld 115, 226

Universal symbol 93

Universe 36, 45, 153, 166, 168, 216, 224

Uterus 102

V

Vegetables 81, 110

Vinci, Leonardo da 43

Violet 67, 156, 158, 159, 161

Visual cortex 20

Volcanoes 129

Von Helmholtz, Hermann 28, 30

Von Leibniz, Gottfried 28

Von Oech, Roger 45, 46

W

Wacky dreams 181

Walpole, Horace 23, 200

Wasps 127, 220

Wealth 22, 27, 47, 58, 65, 89, 91, 93, 112, 123, 124, 130, 131, 133, 136, 145, 147, 158, 159, 160, 169, 176, 178, 185, 220, 224, 225

Wells, HG 136, 166

White 62, 87, 114, 118, 125, 127, 156, 161, 205, 207, 212, 219, 222, 230

Wild animals 92, 109, 121

Wilderness 109, 110, 141, 177, 184

Wilson, Colin 37, 40, 194, 200

Wind 120

Wings 139

Winter 230

Wish-fulfilment 30

Wolf 121, 126, 127, 231

Womb 117

Woolf, Virginia 115

Work 106, 130, 160

Y

Yellow 139, 142, 156, 160, 161, 181, 205, 207, 227, 230, 231

Young, Michael 64

Z

Zodiac 153, 154

Lightning Source UK Ltd.
Milton Keynes UK
UKHW022326091220
374887UK00010B/1966

9 781906 958985